UNDERSTANDING
ALICE ADAMS

UNDERSTANDING CONTEMPORARY AMERICAN LITERATURE

Matthew J. Bruccoli, Founding Editor

Linda Wagner-Martin, Series Editor

UNDERSTANDING

ALICE ADAMS

Bryant Mangum

The University of South Carolina Press

Published by the University of South Carolina Press
Columbia, South Carolina 29208

www.sc.edu/uscpress

Manufactured in the United States of America

28 27 26 25 24 23 22 21 20 19
10 9 8 7 6 5 4 3 2 1

Library of Congress Cataloging-in-Publication Data can be found at
http://catalog.loc.gov/.

ISBN 978-1-61117-933-0 (cloth)
ISBN 978-1-61117-934-7 (ebook)

This book was printed on recycled paper with
30 percent postconsumer waste content.

CONTENTS

SERIES EDITOR'S PREFACE

The Understanding Contemporary American Literature series was founded by the estimable Matthew J. Bruccoli (1931–2008), who envisioned these volumes as guides or companions for students as well as good nonacademic readers, a legacy that will continue as new volumes are developed to fill in gaps among the nearly one hundred series volumes published to date and to embrace a host of new writers only now making their marks on our literature.

As Professor Bruccoli explained in his preface to the volumes he edited, because much influential contemporary literature makes special demands, "the word *understanding* in the titles was chosen deliberately. Many willing readers lack an adequate understanding of how contemporary literature works; that is, of what the author is attempting to express and the means by which it is conveyed." Aimed at fostering this understanding of good literature and good writers, the criticism and analysis in the series provide instruction in how to read certain contemporary writers—explicating their material, language, structures, themes, and perspectives—and facilitate a more profitable experience of the works under discussion.

In the twenty-first century Professor Bruccoli's prescience gives us an avenue to publish expert critiques of significant contemporary American writing. The series continues to map the literary landscape and to provide both instruction and enjoyment. Future volumes will seek to introduce new voices alongside canonized favorites, to chronicle the changing literature of our times, and to remain, as Professor Bruccoli conceived, contemporary in the best sense of the word.

Linda Wagner-Martin, Series Editor

ACKNOWLEDGMENTS

This book originated in conversations I had with Linda Wagner-Martin. I am grateful to her for her continuing encouragement, her support, and her friendship. I also wish to thank Jim Denton and Linda Haines Fogle of the University of South Carolina Press, who offered valuable advice from the moment I began my work on this project. Bill Adams, Suzanne Axland, and Patricia Callahan have gracefully responded to my many queries, and I am most appreciative of their help.

I am deeply indebted to Alice Adams's biographer and my dear friend, Carol Sklenicka, who has been beyond generous in sharing her knowledge, her resources, her time, and her wisdom with me. Alice Adams's son, Peter Linenthal, has been helpful in countless ways, and I am grateful to him for his help and friendship.

David Latané, chair of the English Department at Virginia Commonwealth University, has given me encouragement and all the support I dared ask for during the writing of this book, and I thank him. Montse Fuentes, dean of the College of Humanities and Sciences at Virginia Commonwealth University has generously provided assistance when it was needed most, and I am very appreciative of her support. I have also received valuable help from these friends and colleagues: Gretchen Comba, Thom Didato, Kate Drowne, Maurice Duke, Aíne Norris, Margret Vopel, and James L. W. West III.

My deep thanks go to my research assistants for their work far beyond the call of duty: Christie Maurer located early serial publications of Adams's stories; Chelsea Gillenwater devoted untold hours to finding, copying, and cataloguing hundreds of reviews of Adams's books; Emily Block went behind me on each draft with a sharp editorial eye and improved the manuscript every time she touched it; Annie Persons has gone through every page, offering suggestions that I invariably followed, and she also prepared the index. Finally I want to express appreciation to my children, Skip, Wrenn, and Charlotte, who have provided inspiration at every turn.

CHAPTER 1

Understanding Alice Adams

> I was always serious [about writing]—came from a literary, no that's wrong, a bookish town, Chapel Hill. Being a writer was the best possible thing. Writers were our folk heroes. So I was always serious about being a writer, or to put it negatively, nothing else occurred to me to be.
>
> Alice Adams, Interview with Kay Bonetti (1987)

Alice Boyd Adams (1926–1999) knew from an early age that she would devote her life to writing, though as a very young girl she had planned to become a poet rather than a fiction writer. Between the ages of nine and thirteen she collected dozens of her poems, many of them vividly imagistic nature poems, in a notebook that she labeled on its cover "The Poems of Alice Adams by Alice Adams."[1] By the time she finished her degree at Radcliffe, which she attended from 1943 through 1946, she had begun to devote her energies to writing short stories and sending them out to magazines. Then, in 1966, The New American Library published her first novel, *Careless Love.*

In the 1970s Adams published two novels, *Families and Survivors* (1974) and *Listening to Billie* (1978), and one short story collection, *Beautiful Girl* (1979), through Alfred A. Knopf, which would remain her publisher throughout her entire career. The 1980s were extraordinarily productive years during which Adams published three novels—*Rich Rewards* (1980), *Superior Women* (1984), and *Second Chances* (1988)—and three collections of short stories—*To See You Again* (1982), *Return Trips* (1985), and *After You've Gone* (1989). The 1990s saw the publication of four novels—*Caroline's Daughters* (1991), *Almost Perfect* (1993), *A Southern Exposure* (1995), and *Medicine Men* (1991)—and one collection of stories, *The Last Lovely City* (1999). Her final novel, *After the War* (2000), was published the year after her death.

Adams remained reluctant throughout her career to speak in interviews about general "meanings" or thematic patterns in her work—or about personal philosophical insights that found expression in her fiction. However, in an interview with Kay Bonetti conducted three years after the publication of her most successful novel, *Superior Women* (1984), Adams provided a guiding principle for those new to her fiction. The interviewer made the following general observation about Adams's work and finally posed a question: "It seems to me that one of your major subject matters is the potential of destructiveness and simultaneously the potential of personal growth through love relationships. That seems to be where you think the core of things exists. Can you explain why that is your subject matter?" Adams gave this response: "Not really. . . . I think most of us are chosen by our subject matters. . . . I don't mean to sound mystic or silly about this, but stories come upon one. I don't go around groping for stories. They appear in my mind, so the reasons for those choices are so deep that they have to do with my entire unconscious."[2] With this answer Adams provided both a guide and a challenge for readers approaching the body of her eleven novels and five collections of stories, and she did so without telling readers what themes they should expect to find in her works. Her response suggests three approaches to her work: one is biographical; a second is historical or cultural; and the third is analytical, as it explores the ways in which Adams's thoughts and ideas—conscious and unconscious—reveal themselves in her writing, sometimes reinforcing familiar social and cultural patterns and as often celebrating mystery and wonder.

In her suggestion that, like most writers, she was chosen by her "subject matters," Adams invites readers to consider that the subject matters that chose her included experiences that came to her by chance. The most obvious of these are those experiences that were hers by virtue of her having been born into a family, place, and time that she did not choose, at least for much of her childhood, adolescence, and early adulthood. There were then the later experiences that came to her in adulthood, many of them again through chance rather than choice, by virtue of the zeitgeist of her time—1960s, '70s, '80s, and '90s, those decades of her publishing career. Clearly some events that she wrote about come from details in her life. She drew extensively on her early years in Chapel Hill, North Carolina—her family, her early friendships, the house of her childhood—for material for her fiction. Later her settings often include San Francisco, where she lived from 1949 until her death, and Mexico, which she visited virtually every year of her life from the late 1960s forward and about which she published a "travel companion," *Mexico: Some Travels and Some Travelers There* (1990). As she points out in interviews, biographical details often provide a framework for her stories or novels, though she cautions readers that biographical details in her life are, for her, typically only a starting point in the artistic process. In an interview she was asked about the relationship of "any [Adams] short story to an actual occurrence in the world." Adams's response was that "most typically [the story originates in] my own experience, and I give that experience to someone else."[3]

Biography

One way to enter Alice Adams's fictional world is through those biographical details that were important to her as she encountered them or that left a stamp on her psyche. Born in Fredericksburg, Virginia, on August 14, 1926, Adams soon moved with her parents to Chapel Hill, North Carolina, where her father, Nicholson Barney Adams, known as "Nic," had taken a faculty position teaching Spanish at the University of North Carolina. In 1932 Adams's father had to be hospitalized for nervous exhaustion, the beginning of a pattern of depressions and "nervous breakdowns" for Nic Adams that also plague several of the father figures in Adams's work. During the summers of 1934 and 1935 Nic Adams had a flirtation with Dotsie Wilson, who, with her husband Tom, had been visiting the Adams family at their summer camp near Sebago Lake, in Maine. The strain this placed on the Adams-Wilson family friendship was felt by all involved for years, and the effect on Agatha Adams of the flirtation between Nic Adams and Dotsie Wilson shows up often in Alice's fiction. Nic Adams later married Dotsie Wilson after Agatha's death, in 1950, at the age of fifty-seven.

In her eleventh year Adams made one of the most important friendships of her life with Judith Clark (later Judith Adams), who moved with her parents from Wisconsin by way of Connecticut to Chapel Hill in 1937. The Adams-Clark friendship remained strong from their initial meeting, through their time together at Chapel Hill High School, and until Adams's death. Adams spent the 1940–1941 academic year, her final year in public school, at Wisconsin High School in Madison, Wisconsin, where Nic Adams had received a visiting academic appointment at the University of Wisconsin. In the fall of the next year Adams entered St. Catherine's, a private Episcopal girl's school in Richmond, Virginia, which she did not like but at which she experienced success as literary editor of the St. Catherine's yearbook. She entered Radcliffe College in the summer of 1943 and accumulated many of the experiences that she would include in *Superior Women* (1984), commercially her most successful book and the book for which she is best known. Also during her Radcliffe years she formed a close relationship with Trummy Young, an accomplished African American trombonist from Savannah, Georgia, and Richmond, Virginia, who played with Benny Goodman, Charlie Parker, Dizzy Gillespie, and Louis Armstrong. In her final year at Radcliffe Adams met Mark Linenthal, and they were married on November 30, 1946, just months after Adams's twentieth birthday.

After Mark received a graduate degree from Harvard, the Linenthals traveled to Europe to attend the Salzburg Global Seminar. Their European trip included stays in Italy, Spain, and France, providing Adams with details—settings and characters—that she would later use in her fiction. Back in the United States, the Linenthals settled in California, where Mark enrolled in graduate school at Stanford and where Adams met William ("Billy") Abrahams, who became a lifelong friend and supporter of Adams as a fiction writer. From almost the beginning, the Adams-Linenthal marriage was an unhappy one. By the time of Agatha Adams's death, in 1950, Alice Adams had begun considering seriously her wish to be single and to be a writer. Then, soon after the birth, in 1951, of Adams's son, Peter Linenthal, whom she "loved/liked/was crazy about . . . on sight . . . a whole other story,"[4] her life turned in the direction of pursuing her career as a professional writer. By 1958, as she puts it, "my son was seven and it was increasingly clear to me that his father and I were making each other very unhappy. But we had no money, and I did not see how I could leave. Still an unpublished writer, I was not a good job prospect. However, I decided to go back 'home,' to North Carolina, for that summer."[5]

As it turned out, that summer of 1958 was one of the most important turning points for Adams both personally and professionally. Her return trip to Chapel Hill allowed her to reconnect with the town and region of her youth, and it gave her "a pleased sense of being, now, in my own small hometown, a grown-up, at last, a woman among women."[6] It also provided her an opportunity to meet two people who would come to be among the most important friends in her life. The first was Dr. Lucie Jessner, a professor of psychiatry at the University of North Carolina Medical School. Through Lucie Jessner, Adams met Henry Maxwell ("Max") Steele, with whom Adams had an intense romantic relationship in the summer of 1958.[7] The professional turning point of Adams's life came near the end of the summer when she received word that her story "Winter Rain" had been accepted for publication by *Charm*. It was her first acceptance, and, as she explained it in a 1984 interview, the sale of that story "gave me the courage to get a divorce." It also created the illusion for her that "I would sell every story I wrote," which "of course . . . didn't happen."[8] However, the course of her career as a literary artist who was also a professional writer—and as it turned out a very successful one—was from that point set.

Back in San Francisco in 1959, she ended her marriage to Mark Linenthal in October, and she later began a love affair with Vasco Pereira, a married Portuguese consul to the United States living in San Francisco. Adams's affair with Pereira, painful as it was emotionally for Adams, became one of the most important events in Adams's life professionally. By caricaturing Pereira in her portrait of Pablo Valdespina in *Careless Love* and satirizing Daisy's obsession with him, Adams gained experience as a writer in learning to distance herself from biographical material very close to her.

In 1964 Adams met the San Francisco interior designer Robert McNie, with whom she would live for two decades. McNie played a prominent role in Adams's fiction as a prototype for Richard Fallon, the brilliant, unpredictable, and ultimately tragically doomed lover of Stella Blake in *Almost Perfect*. In the course of Adams's long relationship with McNie she met many individuals who were part of his social set and who came to play supporting roles in various stories and novels. Adams and McNie took annual trips to Mexico, the setting of which not only forms the basis for details in *Mexico: Some Travels and Some Travelers There* but also works its way into a number of her stories, most obviously "La Señora" and "Mexican Dust."

Toward the end of the 1980s, after her relationship with McNie ended and as Adams entered her sixties, she began reaching out in several different directions for fictional subjects. For *Medicine Men* (1997) she drew on her cancer diagnosis and the treatment she received for it in 1992. For *A Southern Exposure* (1995), the novel immediately preceding *Medicine Men,* and for her final novel, *After the War* (2000), a sequel to *A Southern Exposure* that was published posthumously, Adams returned for her primary setting to the place that had played such an important role in her life and in her previous fiction, a small North Carolina town she calls Pinehill. It is a town very close geographically to the fictional Hilton, which is a thinly disguised Chapel Hill. Adams's return to the South in two of her last three novels points to a truth that her formative years in Chapel Hill were important in her fiction writing from beginning to end. As she says in the fictional "Home Is Where," "I needed to return to a place where I had been young."[9] Her return to Pinehill in her last works suggests that perhaps the South was where she was finally most at home in her fiction, though it was not a place to which she ever wanted to return to live.

Subjects and Major Themes

As the author of eleven novels and five short story collections containing seventy-seven of her published stories, Adams was a prolific novelist and short story writer. In interviews she spoke of typically having a story—the "form" she often admitted she loved best—in progress as she was working on a novel or a novel in progress as she was writing a story, switching back and forth between the two in the course of her usual writing day. During her lifetime she won high praise for her work in both genres, receiving recognition for her novels from the National Book Critics Circle and from numerous reviewers. The critical recognition she received for her short stories was even more impressive: she was the recipient of the O. Henry Award for short fiction twenty-three times, winning first prize six times and sharing the honor of receiving an O. Henry lifetime achievement award with only Joyce Carol Oates, John Updike, and Alice Munro. She also won three Best American Short Stories awards.

From the reviews of Adams's work that appeared after the publication of each of her books and from the few scholarly assessments of her fiction, the general opinion prevails that Adams's major contribution to American letters—the thing for which she will most likely be remembered—is her achievement in the genre of short fiction. And while it is true that to many readers her most memorable works—masterpieces such as "The Swastika on Our Door," "Roses, Rhododendron," "Beautiful Girl," "A Pale and Perfectly Oval Moon," and "The Last Lovely City," for example—are short stories, this fact should not diminish the importance of her achievements as a novelist or lead the reader to underestimate the interdependence of her work in the two genres. Adams was considered an astute cultural historian and social satirist from the beginning to the end of her career as a novelist. Grover Sales, after reading her third novel, called her the "Boswell of our neurotic intelligentsia,"[10] and the perceptiveness of the social commentary of her novels is not infrequently compared to that of Jane Austen. In Adams's case, the years of her writing life coincide with such major cultural, social, and political phenomena as the second-wave feminist movement, the civil rights movement, the gay rights movement, the Vietnam war protests, the Watergate hearings, and the Iran-Contra scandal. Adams's novels examine ways in which the social and political forces associated with these phenomena often determine the ways in which her characters face their personal dilemmas. In the process of contextualizing the characters' conflicts relative to particular social phenomena of their time, Adams's novels when taken together create a narrative that is a cultural history of four of the most complex and turbulent decades in our history: the 1960s, '70s, '80s, and '90s.

Adams was always a champion of gender equality, and it is little surprise that many or most of the central characters—the heroes—in her novels are women. Her novels typically depict the struggle toward self-sufficiency of the post–World War II woman at various points in her struggle for independence, exploring the cultural changes of this era in a manner similar to the way F. Scott Fitzgerald's fiction documented the evolution of the new woman of the post–War I era. Adams anticipated in her characters the complexities that would accompany increased freedom and independence for women in the decades following the end of World War II: they resist the roles assigned them in the patriarchal order; they seek self-realization outside the spheres of motherhood and homemaking; they have sexual encounters outside marriage and are confronted with moral dilemmas related to these encounters in the face of centuries of social and gender constructions that have prohibited such relationships; they have strained marriages that often end in divorce; women with children enter the workforce; and they become politically active. In each of her eleven novels Adams examines the lives of women who are moving toward or attempting to move toward self-realization as they fulfill their responsibilities—responsibilities of child rearing, responsibilities of friendship, responsibilities of prior commitment.

One of the reasons Adams gave for continuing to enjoy novel-writing even when her stories continued to receive more extravagant praise was that "there are certain issues that simply cannot be addressed in short stories."[11] These "issues" would have included frank discussions of sexuality or of open rebellion against the patriarchal establishment—issues that would have been too controversial for some magazines to which Adams would be submitting her stories. The novel as a genre allowed Adams freedom, space, and latitude to explore the evolution of her "new-woman" heroines, and even if the novels were viewed solely as carefully observed, sharp social commentary on an important era in American culture—and they are much more than this artistically—her eleven novels are a valuable part of her literary legacy and of American cultural history.

The novels are of major importance in establishing the path the Alice Adams heroine travels from her earliest incarnations to her last; this, in turn, allows readers to contextualize individual stories from Adams's short story canon. This path establishes a thematic arc over Adams's fiction, and it has divisions that break roughly along decade lines and markers that correspond to broad thematic shifts. The early novels and stories—those of the 1960s and 1970s, that is, those in the first segment of the arc—introduce the subjects that concerned Adams throughout her career—romantic love, family, work, friendship, and nostalgia among them. Thematically, however, there is a clear privileging by her heroines of romantic ideals and romantic love in the first novels and earliest stories. Adams's heroines concern themselves most with romantic love, even as they experience work as a means of achieving self-sufficiency and independence.

The main characters of the 1980s works, those in the second segment of the thematic arc, generally maintain their romantic ideals and a strong romantic sensibility, but they begin to understand that one's self-esteem—one's move toward autonomy—likely depends more on finding work that one loves than on becoming attached to a man, regardless of the strength in the moment of any romantic relationship. The main characters in these middle works of the 1980s sometimes look back to times when their lives were different, and they use nostalgia for various psychological ends, even as they look ahead to a time when they will become almost old—a time when friendship often trumps romantic love. In the works of the final segment of the arc, works of the 1990s, the main characters do not lose sight of their romantic ideals or their belief in work as an important part of their identity, but they become more circumspect, dealing with the realities of becoming older by attaching increasing value to friendship and by looking forward to their independence in the near future, even as they look ahead to a time in the more distant future when their children—the next generation—will occupy center stage in American culture.

As is true of her novels, the focus in most of Adams's short stories is on women's struggle toward independence in the post–War II period; as in the novels, the settings of the stories range from the American South and Northeast to the American West and, in her later stories, Mexico. From her first work—whether story or novel—to her last, Adams's central thematic concern is with exploring ways in which her characters are able to break free of those things that deprive them of individual freedom—and ways that they can become individuated, autonomous women. What distinguishes Adams's short stories from her novels is principally the compression and sharp focus of the stories, qualities that her novels frequently lack, carried as they often are by complex story lines and involving, as they often do, many characters. The stories are primarily character-driven; they typically point the reader toward a central dramatic conflict. The details of the stories are compressed through artful layering of the thematic strands of the narratives. By considering the stories against the backdrop of the novels, the reader gains insight into the process by which Adams created in story after story, volume after volume, powerful narratives that are thematically rich and stylistically lyrical—narratives that place Adams, as many have observed, in the company of such great American writers as Joyce Carol Oates, Flannery O'Conner, John Cheever, and F. Scott Fitzgerald, among many others.

Influences and Narrative Style

Adams was reluctant to speak about influences on her writing. She did, however, cite Joyce Carol Oates as "a tremendous influence," and she noted that Cynthia Ozick and Diane Johnson were also writers she greatly admired, adding that "all three of those women I've just mentioned are very unlike me but I'd say they've all been influences."[12] Although Adams resisted giving examples of the specific ways in which other writers influenced her in her own writing, a casual remark Adams made very near the end of her life suggests a particular affinity between her work and that of F. Scott Fitzgerald. In late April 1999, about a month before her death and about the time she was having knee problems that required surgery, Adams had dinner with the writer John ("Jack") Leggett, who was a former director of the Iowa Writer's Workshop. She told him over dinner, "[F. Scott Fitzgerald's] 'The Rich Boy' is maybe the best story I ever read."[13] Leggett went back home, read the story again, and then called Adams to express his surprise that she held the story in such high regard. He told her "it seemed more like a sort of an outline for a novel." Leggett proceeded to characterize "The Rich Boy" as going "from the beginning of this man's [Anson Hunter's] life to his death." Then he summarized the plot for Adams, concluding with the remark that "it's sort of formless, you know?" Adams responded with the last words about writing she ever spoke to him: "But Jack! You know I don't care for plot at all."[14]

Setting aside for the moment the elegance of Fitzgerald's prose, to which Adams's prose is often compared in reviews of her work, it is easy to see features of Fitzgerald's narrative style in "The Rich Boy" that Adams would have found appealing and closely akin to her own narrative style. She was more interested in the unique way Fitzgerald revealed the character of Anson Hunter than she was with the linear plot line of "The Rich Boy." Technically the story is a first-person narrative, not the point of view that Adams most often chose for her novels or her stories, but Fitzgerald gave his narrator in this story the same kind of omniscience that Adams used in her close third-person narratives—narratives that are often quite long, stretching over decades, and narratives in which there are frequent shifts back and forth in the focus of narration, as is true in "The Rich Boy." Ten of Adams's eleven novels are written from a third-person point of view; only one (*Rich Rewards*) is a first-person narrative. Fifty-seven of the short stories in her five collections are written in the third person; twenty are from a first-person perspective.

Adams frequently gives readers what Annie Gottlieb characterized as an omniscience "occasionally smacking of Olympian mischief,"[15] which Adams achieves, among other ways, by dropping into the middle of a third-person linear narrative parenthetical asides that suggest the narrator behind the actual narrative understands more than any of the characters do at that particular time. She gives the reader a sense of "roominess and space" as well as of "compactness of character"—qualities that her editor Victoria Wilson saw in her work from the beginning and qualities that Adams, no doubt, saw in Fitzgerald's work, particularly "The Rich Boy."[16] Like Fitzgerald, Adams demonstrates in novel after novel and story after story the ability to subordinate plot to character and to create a sense in the reader, again in Gottlieb's words, "of seeing human lives and relationships *across time*."[17]

CHAPTER 2

The Early Novels

Careless Love, Families and Survivors, and *Listening to Billie*

Careless Love (1966)

In her early novels Adams built a foundation for subjects and themes she spent her life as a writer developing and refining, and these are very much in evidence in her first novel, *Careless Love,* published in 1966 by New American Library. The English edition was published the following year by Constable as *The Fall of Daisy Duke* (Adams's originally proposed title). Though its contemporary American critical reception was unenthusiastic, *Careless Love* is a sophisticated foundational work that contains the seeds of virtually all of Adams's later works. From the standpoint of social and cultural history, *Careless Love* treats the plight of post–War II women, who by the 1950s and 1960s found divorce to be an available and socially acceptable alternative to living in a loveless marriage, an option that had been infrequently exercised by women in the post–War I period. Even those women in the 1920s who had on the surface gained a high degree of individual freedom—flappers, for example—were still likely, in the words of one of F. Scott Fitzgerald's early Jazz Age heroines, destined to board "the sinking ship of future matrimony,"[1] anchored economically in the patriarchy; women's escape through means other than marriage remained slim. In the post–War II period of *Careless Love,* divorce was a socially acceptable choice available to the novel's main character, Daisy Duke; and it is her divorce that allows her, in the end, to evolve into a stronger and wiser person. Virtually all of Adams's novels and many of her stories are concerned with the benefits as well as the difficulties and complexities associated with divorce.

Careless Love also addresses the subject of the importance of work, particularly in the lives of women who are attempting to establish identities apart from men, whether these men are their present or estranged husbands or their lovers. Work becomes in the end a major component of Daisy's redemption in *Careless Love* when she at last takes a job in an art gallery. Also, through Daisy Duke, Adams establishes her enduring concern with the importance of family and family dynamics, particularly regarding the role that mother-daughter and father-daughter relationships play in the lives of daughters, both in childhood and after they have moved into adulthood. In Daisy's case, the suicide of her mother shapes the way she thinks about possible ways of dealing with overwhelming emotions such as despair. Similarly, the presence of a father like Ran Duke, who is emotionally detached, exerts a powerful influence on the way Daisy interacts with men.

It is clear from its treatment of such subjects as divorce, the role of work in the public sphere for women, and family relationships in the America of the 1960s that *Careless Love* has "a superb sense of social milieu," as the dust jacket of the British edition maintains. However, the subject at the heart of *Careless Love* is love, and the way Adams deals with this subject is a crowning achievement of the novel. In her treatment of Daisy's obsession with Pablo Valdespina, a stereotypical Latin lover, it is clear that Adams is satirizing the extremes of self-pity often experienced by a rejected lover. Beneath the caricature and satire, however, is Adams's serious interrogation of the subject of romantic love. Daisy has a kind of double vision that allows her finally both to accept the idea that perhaps she has genuinely loved Pablo and at the same time to acknowledge that what she has felt may not have been love at all. Adams establishes Daisy at the beginning as an idealist who, "even more than most women . . . lived for love" (13). Her belief at the beginning of the novel before her divorce is that love is not simply a construct but is more likely an absolute, a mystery that must be experienced rather than known through the intellect, an idea that Adams explores in many of her stories.

Daisy finally concludes she must challenge the institution of marriage when it is a relationship without love; she is in what she considers such a marriage. When Joseph, her husband, counters her wish to get a divorce by saying "but I love you" (12), she exercises the power of her conviction and essentially subverts the patriarchal order, going forward with the divorce so that she can search for love. After she and Pablo find what both characterize as a "miracle" in their love of each other only to have it end with Pablo's decision that they cannot have a life together, Daisy is never quite able to dismiss the possibility that she has experienced the mystery of love, although she discovers in the end that Pablo has likely been disingenuous in his claim that he loved her exclusively. Adams presents Daisy's case for the possibility that romantic love is a reality that transcends understanding through rational means.

In the end, Adams renders her interrogation of the subject of romantic love in *Careless Love* sophisticated through the use of irony and satire. The subject is one that becomes a trademark stamp in Adams's work, present in one form or another in virtually every novel and most of the short stories that Adams wrote from 1966 until her death. As Beverly Lowry, writing almost twenty years after the publication of *Careless Love* in a review of Adams's third short story collection, *Return Trips* (1985), noted, "nobody writes better about falling in love than Alice Adams."[2] What Lowry does not say is that each time Adams approaches the subject, she does so freshly, rarely judging her characters who have ideas often quite different from Daisy's or from cultural norms related to love, falling in love, or the role of love in marriage. Women in Adams's later novels and stories embrace a variety of attitudes toward love and marriage that differ from Daisy's, but Adams's strong women—her heroines, the women she admires—always share a belief in the need for reciprocity and equality in relationships, whatever their attitudes about the life or death of romantic love in their individual worlds.

Families and Survivors (1974)

The years between 1966 and 1974, the year of publication of *Families and Survivors,* were good years for Adams, both personally and professionally. Perhaps oddly, this had very little to do with the fact that she published *Careless Love* in 1966—the year that she turned forty—and much more to do with her discovery of a romantic partner and with her success in being able finally to write and publish her short stories. As she put it in one interview occasioned by the publication of *Families and Survivors,* "I think I probably am a good example of life begins at forty—I'm forty-eight—[those eight years after forty] have all been a vast improvement. I began to come together after a long period of floundering."[3] In 1964 she met Robert McNie, with whom she had lived ten years when *Families and Survivors* was published, and her stories at long last began to appear in places such as *Cosmopolitan* and *Redbook.* With the *New Yorker*'s publication of "Gift of Grass" in 1969 and "Ripped Off" and "The Swastika on Our Door" in 1971, Adams began to gain a reputation as a short story writer. Her determination to pursue the short story form with renewed vigor after the publication of *Careless Love* came from her disappointment with the novel's reception: she thought that perhaps novel writing was not for her and that she "might do better learning how to write short stories."[4]

Her renewed focus on short stories after *Careless Love* was a fortunate one since the reputation Adams had earned—particularly through her stories in the *New Yorker*—after the publication of the novel led indirectly to Knopf's acceptance, in 1973, of *Families and Survivors.* Victoria Wilson, the Knopf editor who would become Adams's editor from 1973 until Adams's death, knew her by reputation as a *New Yorker* short story writer before the *Families and Survivors* manuscript crossed her desk. In her praise of the manuscript, Wilson attributed much of its success to Adams's effectiveness as a writer of short stories: "All of the things you use when writing short stories—that compactness of character and yet that feeling of roominess and space is brought to the novel."[5] Adams turned what she later described as essentially thirteen related stories into a highly acclaimed novel, and she gave much credit for the success of its form to Wilson.

With the publication of *Families and Survivors,* Adams joined the company, in Billy Abrahams's words, of "John Updike, Mary McCarthy, Louis Auchincloss and Alison Lurie, novelists whose subjects are the manners and morals of the upper-middle and professional classes, and whose characters are concerned less with making a living than with making a life." Reviewers of *Families and Survivors* picked up on many of those qualities that came to characterize Adams's fiction over the next twenty-five years. The "compactness of character" that Wilson referred to is particularly evident in Adams's treatment of Louisa Calloway, the novel's central character, whose life the reader follows from 1941 to 1971. Through close third-person omniscient narration, Adams allows the reader access to Louisa's views of events as she is experiencing them in the present moment but also comments (usually parenthetically) on how she would look back on them from some point in the future. This method allows the reader to see "human lives and relationships *across time,*" giving the feeling of roominess that Wilson spoke of, but it also has the effect of compressing much information about Louisa into the small space of "essential scenes."

What Adams accomplishes in a rather slim, two-hundred-page novel is a representation of the complicated story of a main character's movement toward strength and independence over a thirty-year period in which virtually all of the details come together in a mosaic of contemporary American life. The novel's last chapter provides a study in miniature of the method Adams uses to accomplish this. At the time of this chapter—New Year's Eve 1970—Louisa has married John, a friend from her teenage years with whom she fell in love on the occasion of his appearance at her father's funeral years ago. In this final chapter Louisa and John have attended a New Year's Eve party at the communal home of Louisa's daughter Maude and her friends and housemates. Through this celebration and through other parties going on at the same time and described by the omniscient narrator, Adams provides a snapshot of the complex and often confusing contemporary life lived by the adults—the parents—and their children who had been a part of Louisa's life for many years. The original adults of the novel, most of whom have divorced and remarried, are all having parties in nearby locations, and the children of the original couples, most of them young adults themselves now, are making the rounds of their reconfigured families. Sally and Andrew's daughter, Jennifer Magowan, now dating Kate and David's son Stephen, must visit a pretentious gathering at the home of Jennifer's mother, Grace, and her now-husband Martin, the gay brother of Louisa's first husband, Michael. Then Jennifer and Stephen must also pay a visit to the party given by her father, Alex, and his now-wife Sally, originally married to Andrew, who is, at the moment, vacationing in Jamaica with his second wife, Isabel, his former student. Jennifer must explain to her father why sister-daughter Alison has been left in the care of the beautiful and level-headed Maude, daughter of Louisa, in the communal house where Alison, on leave from a California treatment center for emotionally disturbed individuals, has fallen asleep after drinking too much wine.

After leaving Maude's party and while the other parties are in progress, Louisa and her husband, John, are heading to their home alone in the hills beyond Berkeley, and Adams allows the reader to see them in a quiet, thoughtful moment that is in sharp contrast to the chaotic scene they have just left. Louisa, now a successful painter, is relieved to have escaped a gathering where relationships among members of both the older and the younger generations are puzzling to her, though she continues to be curious, open-minded, and determined to grow from all experiences she encounters. She asks John, "But which boy was Maude *with*?" (195). He assures her that she doesn't have to be with anyone, suggesting that there has been a generational shift in attitudes toward love and sex. Louisa is, however, preoccupied with her own ideas about these subjects. As she reflects on her relationship with John in the past, she worries that "she and John don't talk," though she acknowledges that they do often still "make love" (193). At other times and "in other moods she romanticizes their relationship, and she tells herself that their lengthy frame of reference makes talk unnecessary—simply to be together is to communicate." Then, back home, tonight they are talking a lot, and they do have sex. Moving into the future (and revealed in parentheses), Louisa asks herself if love relationships in which partners talk to each other and also have sex are possible: "(Perhaps both are true?)" (193). Her ideas about love, sex, and friendship are continuing to evolve.

In her review of *Families and Survivors,* Margaret Manning observed that all of the characters in the novel, not just Louisa, are searching for love.[6] They are all also searching to find ways to live their lives free of controlling relationships, ways of surviving in a world in which traditional family life has changed dramatically, ways of integrating work into their lives in a manner that gives their lives meaning, and ways of maintaining friendship in a relationship where there is also passion. In the end, *Families and Survivors* presents a painstakingly detailed picture of life in contemporary America that engages all of these subjects and themes that will find their way into virtually all of Adams's short stories and novels from *Families and Survivors* forward.

Listening to Billie (1978)

Alice Adams's third novel, *Listening to Billie* was published in 1978. At the time of the novel's release, Adams had already been known for many years as a successful short story writer through her contributions to the *New Yorker, Atlantic Monthly, Redbook, McCall's,* and the *Paris Review.* Her stories had also appeared in seven of the O. Henry Award collections leading up to *Listening to Billie,* and her second novel, *Families and Survivors,* had been nominated alongside books by Saul Bellow, Larry Woiwode, E. L. Doctorow, and William Kotzwinkle for the 1975 National Book Critics Circle best fiction award, won that year by Doctorow for his novel *Ragtime.* In her lead-in to a *Publisher's Weekly* interview with Adams shortly after the publication of *Listening to Billie,* Patricia Holt observed, "Now, with [the] publication of 'Listening to Billie' . . . it appears likely that Alice Adams is writing her way into a celebrated career,"[7] which, in fact, turned out to be true.

Many reviewers noted in Eliza, the novel's main character, a subtle evolution of "the Alice Adams woman." The stages of Eliza's journey are shown in a series of references to the life and music of the novel's title character, Billie Holiday, who died at the age of forty-four from complications related to cirrhosis of the liver after years of drug and alcohol abuse. Billie Holiday dominates the novel's opening scene, in which a group is gathered in a Greenwich Village nightclub waiting for her entrance as the jukebox plays her songs. Billie "suddenly" makes a grand entrance from the street side "like anyone else. Or not like anyone else at all: she is more beautiful, more shining, holding her face forward like a flower, bright-eyed and smiling, high yellow cheekbones, white teeth and cream-white gardenia at her ear" (3). She is accompanied by her manager and her Great Dane, who has bitten the manager's hand on their way to the club and made them late. Sitting in the club is Eliza Hamilton with her then-boyfriend, Evan Quarles, and she is preoccupied with the near certainty that she is pregnant with Evan's child, though during the evening she also becomes entranced by Billie and the image of Billie's coming into the club accompanied by her wounded manager and her dog. The image becomes indelible: "Eliza retained that scene of Billie's entrance, and Billie singing. . . . She kept it somewhere in her mind; she brought it out and stared at it as she might a stone, something opalescent" (4). The opening scene and Eliza's later viewing it from alternative angles point to the scene's significance and to its resonance as it continues to accumulate meaning from chapter to chapter. Eliza's progress toward self-assurance and independence through the fifteen years of the novel is set against her changing attitude toward this scene and toward Billie's blues.

After Evan's suicide and after her move to California, Eliza is without a man for a time, and she tells herself that she is safe and comfortable with her "delightful small daughter for company" (10). And then, years later, after the summer that "Billie Holiday died, or killed herself, was killed," Eliza "reacted to [Billie's] death in a violent, personal way" (10). She consciously does not play Billie's records, but "sometimes, with a morbid insistence, they came over the radio, unbidden" (11). The "violent, personal way" she reacts to Billie's death becomes most apparent during an encounter with a man who tries to force himself sexually on Eliza, during which time a Billie Holiday song with the following words happens to come "unbidden" over the radio: "I've got a right to sing the blues, I've got a right to moan and sigh" (13). Hearing this, Eliza faces the helplessness of her plight in the situation with a man who is physically stronger than she is, and she concedes to him that she is helpless, prompting him to leave her house in shame without having sex. After the scene with this man, Eliza at last consciously faces the sadness and isolation she has carried inside since Evan's suicide: "Alone, hunched up in her large bed . . . Eliza did not cry, although that was certainly what a part of her would have liked to do; she sensed that somewhere within her there was a woman weeping, or perhaps it was a terrified child, its heart already broken" (13). This acceptance of her sadness becomes the beginning point of Eliza's movement toward freedom and independence.

This is only the first of many steps in Eliza's movement toward independence and self-sufficiency—ironically, also her movement away from identification with those self-destructive aspects of Billie Holiday that led to Billie's early death. Eliza's salvation comes ultimately through her commitment to her work, which is the work of a dedicated poet who labors to refine her art in the hope that it might become the source of her livelihood. The process is a slow and complex one. It begins with Eliza's resolve to pursue her writing seriously, which results in her creation of a poem that is accepted by the *Nation*. This is followed by Eliza's decision to convert Catherine's old room into a writing room for herself, a plan that results in a dispute with Catherine, who is now pregnant and wants a place to store her things or perhaps even a place to live with her baby when it arrives. Soon Eliza's dedication to her work leads to a publication in *Gotham,* a magazine that pays well, suggesting that Eliza may eventually be able to earn a living through her writing.

Through carefully chosen scenes in *Listening to Billie,* Adams takes the reader through the subtle changes in Eliza's character that, in the end, position her in relation to many of Adams's familiar and evolving subjects and themes, many of which will be explored in her stories: the importance of friendship, as Eliza develops a close friendship with a writer-friend Jane; the place of a mother in the life of her daughter, as Eliza assumes an important role in her relationship with Catherine, a role that grants both mother and daughter independence; the importance of sex in love, as Eliza's relationship with Harry evolves into one based on passion and loving friendship; and the importance of work, which Adams finally regards as Eliza's salvation. In an interview on *Listening to Billie,* Adams provided insight into her thoughts about the importance of work for modern women: "What I was interested in writing about in this book was the idea of women getting to work. . . . It seems to me there has been too much about women and their endless problems with the kind of addictive love affair that is so all-consuming it makes sex an excuse for delaying the things that matter like getting to work."[8]

Adams always had the idea that work is important for the development of women's independence and self-esteem. However, in *Listening to Billie* she began to show the central rather than peripheral role that work plays in an individual's pursuit of autonomy. In one of the few scholarly articles on Adams, "Succeeding in Their Times: Alice Adams on Women and Work," Cara Chell argues, "Eliza deliberately survives. She mends herself. She stops listening to the voice of victims and tells herself how to be healed [through work]."[9] At the end of the novel Eliza finally says to Harry, "I'll be glad to get back"—with the implication that she means "back to work." Harry responds, "me, too. It's time for me to do some work. . . . Shall we make a bargain? Both work our heads off this fall and if it goes well . . . we'll go to Mexico" (214), a proposition that emerges from *Listening to Billie* as a prescription for success, both for Adams's heroine and for the man she loves.

In her first three novels Adams introduces the main subjects that she will come back to many times over the course of her career: love, loss, home and family, divorce, friendship, and work—all of these subjects viewed in relation to their role in the movement toward independence of her main characters. Within each of the trio of her first novels her heroines experience changes in their attitudes toward those things that best serve them in their quest for increased self-esteem and autonomy. At the end of *Careless Love,* Daisy Duke has greater insight into her attitudes about romantic love than she did at the beginning, and she has begun to value her work in the art gallery; Louisa Calloway at the close of *Families and Survivors* not only has reevaluated her thoughts about love and family, she has also moved toward the knowledge that her work as an artist is of central importance to her identity; and Eliza Quarles, whose work has come to be at the center of her life, has found that through her work she has gained not only freedom from her fears about suicide but also the self-esteem that will allow her to have a romantic relationship in which she is an equal. Between the first novel of this sequence and the third, there is also a progression from one main character to the next toward greater self-knowledge and personal growth. Adams's short stories published between *Careless Love* and *Listening to Billie*—between 1966 and 1979—were collected in *Beautiful Girl*, her first story collection, and her concerns in these stories often mirror those of the first three novels.

CHAPTER 3

Early Stories

Beautiful Girl

By her admission Adams alternated on any given writing day between novel writing and story writing, often going back and forth between work on a novel during one part of the day and work on a story during another. It is, therefore, no surprise that her novels share subjects and themes with her short stories. It may have come as a surprise, however, to those who had followed her career as a successful novelist with three novels to her credit during the early part of her career when *Beautiful Girl* (1979), her first story collection, appeared in 1979 that short fiction was her favorite genre. As she told Neil Feineman, "The short story is the form I love best."[1] And, as Grover Sales noted in a review of *Listening to Billie,* her "stories in *The New Yorker* and *Atlantic*" had at that time been "represented in every O. Henry Award Collection for the past eight years [building for her a reputation] as an acute social observer with a lucid intelligence, needling wit and instantly recognizable style."[2] The majority of contemporary reviewers had similarly positive feelings about Adams's writing and gave *Beautiful Girl* ringing endorsements, Patricia Holt concluding that "the book is a banquet of riches."[3]

Many reviewers singled out for praise Adams's treatment in the stories of romantic love, loss, family, and work, subjects that are also at the center of her early novels. Susan Wood, in a review that focused on thematic concerns of the collection, became the first critic to sketch a path to the heart of virtually all of Adams's short fiction, in both *Beautiful Girl* and, prophetically as it turns out, all of the later story collections. In "Stories of Love and Loss" (a title that could easily be applied to Adams's first three novels, taken together), Wood established a foundation for considering Adams one those rare post–War II writers with a commitment to Romantic idealism, which Lionel Trilling, as Wood noted, described as "the Romantic fantasy, descended from the Renaissance, of personal ambition and heroism, of life committed to, or thrown away for, some ideal of self."[4] Trilling designated F. Scott Fitzgerald as the last notable American writer to affirm Romantic idealism, which is perhaps most completely realized in Jay Gatsby, who "sprang from his Platonic conception of himself" (*The Great Gatsby* 77) and who had "a romantic readiness such as [Nick had] never found in any other person" (6). Wood used a brief summary of "Beautiful Girl" as her opening exhibit to suggest how Adams extends Fitzgerald's post–War I Romantic idealism to her own post–World War II era, providing a useful lens through which one can envision how love and loss are associated with the idea of Romantic idealism in several stories in the collection. In the process she positioned Adams in the direct line of Fitzgerald.

In selecting the story "Beautiful Girl" to provide the title for the volume, Adams managed to do several important things. First, she connects the story and the entire collection to the tradition of Romantic idealism; also she introduces in the title story many of the themes that are explored in the other stories in *Beautiful Girl,* particularly those themes clustered around the subjects of loss and love in the lives of each story's main characters. But it is interesting, and perhaps another reason that Adams chose "Beautiful Girl" for the volume's title story, that in "Beautiful Girl" she spotlights the subjects and themes that signal her literary heritage and foregrounds them more dramatically and in a glitzier way than she does in the other stories in the collection. An additional quality of the story that makes it well suited to serve as the title story is that Adams presents in it a cross-continental and across-time perspective that is apparent in many of the stories in the volume in which she not only shifts the action from present to past but also creates a geographical shift typically from the American South (often Chapel Hill, North Carolina) to the far West (most often San Francisco, California). The "beautiful girl" of the title, Ardis Bascombe, as she is depicted in the story-within-the-story of "Beautiful Girl"—that is, the story of young Ardis (who is now living in San Francisco) in a past time, when she lived in North Carolina—is a heroine in the line of Fitzgerald characters such as Judy Jones from "Winter Dreams" and Daisy Fay Buchanan from *Gatsby.* In this story-within-the-story, she is a rich tobacco heiress, who in her days as an enchanted University of North Carolina coed in Chapel Hill is a beauty queen widely sought after by men from the most and the least prestigious fraternities, and by social outsiders like Walpole Greene, who has little chance of any social interaction with Ardis. Greene admires Ardis from a distance in her "immaculate pale clothes: flowered cottons, cashmere cardigans" (146), as she appears first with one man and then another, convincing each one that she is his exclusively. Greene both loves her as the campus golden girl and hates her for the perfunctory attention she pays him, calling him "Wopple" when she chooses to acknowledge his presence on campus at all.

On one occasion, having stayed awake all night, Greene decides in a spirit of self-pity to ride his bike out to Ghimgoul Castle, a gathering place of the social elites, and watch the sunrise from a lookout bench near the Castle. Here he contemplates his complex love-hate feelings about Ardis. Predictably she has been at the party inside Ghimgoul Castle, and she stumbles accidentally and drunkenly upon Greene watching the sunrise. He has an urge to hit her, but, without any knowledge of his violent feelings, she overwhelms him with a kiss tasting of bourbon and utters these words: "I love you, Wopple. . . . I truly and purely do" (147). Though "after that night" their relationship does not change, "he now watche[s] over her as a lover would. With love" (147–48). Greene's Romantic idealization of Ardis becomes from that point unshakeable, and it endures for the twenty years leading into the present time of the story, similar in this way to Dexter Green's idealization of Judy Jones, which endures until the last page of "Winter Dreams." Both Dexter Green and Walpole Greene are in this sense heroes in the Romantic tradition referred to by Trilling and by Wood.

Through Ardis, Adams addresses the kind of romantic idealization that is at the center of *Careless Love,* though in "Beautiful Girl" her treatment of this subject is not satirical. As it turns out in this story, Adams subverts the heroic quest myth that Trilling speaks of as "the Romantic fantasy . . . of life committed to, or thrown away for some ideal of self," a quest for writers of Fitzgerald's time and in eras before the Jazz Age—particularly American writers—that would typically have focused on the male as quester. In "Beautiful Girl" Adams does tell that story of the male, Walpole Greene, who places the female, Ardis Bascombe, on a pedestal and commits considerable energy to thoughts of "having her" as an embodiment of the "ideal."

In the end, however, "Beautiful Girl" is mainly Ardis Bascombe's story. She is the central quester who forms an image of her "ideal self," which is a self that has been socially constructed by a culture that mainly values such things as beauty, wealth, social standing, and popularity—all those things that have made Ardis the enchanted coed that Greene and others came to love at Carolina. After her college days in an enchanted setting where she is idealized, Ardis begins to find all people outside that world boring. Ultimately, after marriage and divorce, she leaves her hometown of Winston-Salem, which bores her, for San Francisco, finally retreating from society there because its members are too boring to spend time with. She prefers keeping her own company with alcohol, living in the squalor of a filthy upscale house in a fashionable part of San Francisco, in the kitchen of which she is looked down upon by a grease-stained portrait of herself as a beautiful young woman. When the story opens, she is shown to have become an irredeemable alcoholic, and it is in the present time that the reader discovers her. She is awaiting the arrival of her former Carolina classmate, Walpole Greene, who has come up in the world socially and financially, though now in his fourth unhappy marriage, and who plans to take Ardis out to dinner. By the story's end Ardis has passed out with her head on the kitchen table, Greene has told her daughter that he plans to help her into a rehabilitation center in Connecticut, and he has leaned down and whispered these words into Ardis's ear: "I want you to be my beautiful girl again—." Ardis raises her head and responds from her drunken stupor, "I am a beautiful girl" (152).

Ardis has identified and fallen in love with her idealized self and has settled into a Romantic fantasy—her life thrown away for some ideal of self. In capturing the seeming glamour of Ardis's early life in the story-within-the story, Adams draws the reader into an understanding of how the sparkle of that life could have been sufficiently seductive to draw others into the Romantic idealization of Ardis in that world—most obviously Greene and then Ardis herself. In telling Ardis's story across time through flashback, Adams connects with the traditional male-centered Romantic quest fantasy that Fitzgerald often wrote about in his fiction and that Trilling identified. She also introduces the reader to a world in which females are seen as questers, though in this case the quest is self-directed. In the process Adams brings the Romantic quest into "the 70s, when our response to history has been not the hedonistic grand gestures of an earlier generation, but a quieter, more muted turning inward."[5] Walpole Greene is no Jay Gatsby; his offer of finding help for Ardis is not an especially grand gesture. And Ardis for her part is not flaming out for all the world to see: she is quietly, drunkenly, going through the motions of trying to resurrect a past that was anchored in a Romantic fantasy.

In the layered narrative of "Beautiful Girl" Adams examines several forms of idealization: in the flashback she tells the story of Greene's romantic "love" of Ardis, and through her use of the story-within-a-story she shows that what qualifies as romantic love in one time may reveal itself to have been something altogether different after years have gone by. In a sense Adams deconstructs the concept of young romantic love in "Beautiful Girl." Also, in Ardis's love of herself, Adams foregrounds a kind of fixation on the idealized self—in Ardis's case, self-love—that is rarely seen in Adams's stories and novels, one that is, when it appears, most often attributed to her minor characters, though in "Beautiful Girl" it is an overarching concern. She also brings into the foreground a consideration of the complex concept of loss, which Adams typically treats—even in those characters most consumed by self-love, like Ardis—by showing some of the warm, human qualities of those who have lost the most and often lost because of their own faults and failings. Though largely self-centered, Ardis is viewed by her youngest daughter early in the story as having in some ways been "a wonderful mother" who had given "terrific birthday parties, presents, and clothes" (144). And the reader sympathizes with Greene, who was an outsider looking into Ardis's enchanted world when he was a university student and who is, in the present, facing the reality that this romanticized world no longer exists if it ever did actually exist. On a superficial level the literal losses in the story, similar to those in the early novels, are obvious: Ardis has lost her youth and beauty, as well as a husband; Greene himself has lost the Ardis of his dreams—lost her from the beginning when he had no chance with her and also in the present when she is no longer his "beautiful girl." In the aftermath of his idealization of Ardis, he has also lost three wives and is in the process of losing a fourth. The collateral losses are particularly heartbreaking because, as the reader sees perhaps more than either of the two main players in the drama, the romantic fantasies of both Ardis and Greene have created losses for others close to them. The ones most obviously affected visibly within the story are Ardis's daughters, both of whom have, in effect, lost a mother.

Although it is tempting to try to group the sixteen stories in *Beautiful Girl* around the title story and into one of various categories, in the end Adams's stories resist easy labeling, which is as Adams wished it to be. As she revealed in an interview, when magazine editors turned down stories because they "didn't sound like me," it infuriated her: "They want you to write the same story,"[6] which was exactly what she was trying not to do. The stories in *Beautiful Girl* are not all "the same story," though all share several things in common: all of the stories have the Alice Adams stamp of Romantic idealization that is evident in the title story and that is, not surprisingly, present in the three early novels; all of them contain some form of loss; and in all of the stories there is evidence of Adams's deeply caring treatment of each of her characters—typically San Franciscans or North Carolinians—even those with whom it is most difficult to sympathize, like Ardis Bascombe.

The first three stories in *Beautiful Girl* come under the heading "The Todds": "Verlie I Say unto You," "Are You in Love?," and "Alternatives." The Todds trilogy formed the foundation of what would ultimately become a series of twelve stories that are among Adams's most memorable and important ones. In these stories, she draws extensively on her experiences of growing up in Chapel Hill, North Carolina, and she examines through them many of the subjects of her early novels—romantic love, family, friendship, loss, and work. The first of the Todd stories, "Verlie" and "Are You in Love?," are set in Hilton, a "small university town in the middle South." "Alternatives," the third story, is set variously in Maine and in San Francisco, but it follows characters from the first two stories thirty years into the future with flashbacks to the Hilton years of the first two stories. Three other stories in the volume are closely related to the Todd stories: "Beautiful Girl," which is set in Chapel Hill in the flashback scene, and "Home Is Where" and "Roses, Rhododendron," both set in small, unnamed southern towns, close in description to Hilton/Chapel Hill. The remaining stories in the Hilton group are scattered through the three later story volumes, some bringing back characters from the Todd stories (for example, "A Southern Spelling Bee" in *To See You Again*) but most involving non-Todd main characters, typically single women who are separated, divorced, or widowed and who are often returning to North Carolina either to visit or to stay. Some have gone on to travel the world and only dream in vivid detail of returning to Hilton, the haunted or enchanted place of their childhood, and the setting Adams draws on in two of her last three novels—*A Southern Exposure* and *After the War.*

In "Verlie I Say unto You" Adams foregrounds Verlie, an "illiterate" black housekeeper who works in the home of a privileged white family in the dominant white, patriarchal culture of a small southern university town, and she becomes the moral center of the story. The Todds—Tom, Jessica, Avery, and Devlin—are lonely as individuals and estranged from one another as members of the family. Tom is a university professor, family patriarch, philandering husband, and bigot, who jokingly tells his white friends about the origin of Verlie's name ("Verily, verily I say unto you" from the biblical book of John) and who sees Verlie in stereotypically racist terms; Jessica is a college-educated mother and wife trapped in a marriage to a man she knows is unfaithful and with whom she can share nothing—a woman whose only happy thoughts in this story are of her past successes in college, when she was much closer to realizing her ideals and when she had friends she could talk to; Avery, an Adams persona, is a bright young girl who witnesses her father kissing a woman not his wife, among many puzzling interactions between other adults her life. She is aware of the disconnections in the family but has no one with whom to share her thoughts and insights since Devlin, Avery's young brother, is fearful of everything and everyone, including Avery.

Verlie goes about her work without self-pity, perhaps because she does actually have work in the financially difficult times of the 1930s. She remains fearful that her physically abusive, wandering husband, Horace, will return and leave her with more scars. But the reader learns in the heart of the story that Verlie is saved by her capacity to love and her belief that love is possible, a truth she discovered when she fell in love with Clifton, a man who occasionally works for the Todds. She is released from her fear of Horace when Tom Todd informs her that Horace has died in Memphis, and she is at that point free to love and be loved by Clifton without fear. The Todds are baffled when Verlie smiles rather than weeps when she receives the news that the abusive Horace is dead. They are doubly surprised when Verlie is devastated and inconsolable after she learns that Clifton has died. Tom Todd remarks with incredulity to Irene McGinnis, with whom he is having a flirtation, "I believe those two people had real affection for each other" (17). After a time of mourning following Clifton's death, Verlie returns to work, though "there is a grayish tinge to the color of her skin that does not go away" (18). In Verlie's world there is such a thing as love, and the loss of it leaves emotional scars. But, as Adams has maintained in virtually all of her fiction to date, work becomes a way of dealing with loss—and of maintaining one's sense of self. Though love and its loss appear not yet to have become part of the lives of any of the Todds, Avery, most directly, and Jessica, indirectly, will deal with both in the future.

While there are hints of Jessica Todd's romantic idealism in her memories of her college self in "Verlie," the second Todd story, "Are You in Love?," demonstrates that she is actually still very much a frustrated dreamer—a romantic idealist—in the present time of her life as mother of Avery and Devlin and as wife of Tom. Though most of the time Jessica, who owns a small bookstore in Hilton and who is "not aging well," sees herself mainly in terms of her defects (her "pores and sags"), she transcends her negative self-image when a young undergraduate with a fascination for poetry flatters her by complimenting her on her hair: "Ma'am," he tells her, "you do have the prettiest hair" (19, 21). The shy, young student, Linton Wheeler, has no romantic interest in Jessica—"He likes Jessica, or, rather, he does not *not* like her, as he does most older women"—but his compliment dominates Jessica's day, sending her into an imagined world in which she and Linton could conceivably become lovers. She thinks back to her girlhood reading of the British Romantics Shelley, Byron, Keats, and Wordsworth, and she begins to imagine Linton's attention as "a glimpse of possibilities, a bright glimpse like a slit in the darkness of her usual melancholy" (22).

Jessica's romantic illusions collide with reality when she arrives home in the afternoon to a scene around the pool where Tom is—as he often is—paying attention to the attractive wife of a couple who have brought their children over for a swim and drinks. Jessica must face the reality of Tom's attraction to the "small and blond" Irene McGinnis as she (Jessica) "wonders how that would be, to be a woman looked at by men, aware of the power of one's face, one's small and desirable body" (25). Avery, who has a crush on Irene's son Harry, pushes him "floundering" into the pool, prompting him to yell at her "You little bitch—" (27). This terrifies Avery and prompts her mother to drag her toward the house, shake her, and yell these words at her: "What's the matter with you, are you in love with Harry McGinnis? *Are you in love?*" (28). Both mother and daughter wind up weeping, and the reader understands the sad truth that Avery cannot know: her mother's extreme reaction comes out of deep despair as she realizes that her own romantic fantasies about "loving" Linton—or of being loved by him or by anyone—have been illusions. The projection of her frustrated dreams onto Avery is an act of despair.

In "Alternatives," the final story about the Todds, many of those qualities that Victoria Wilson praised in Adams's short fiction in her review of the manuscript of *Families and Survivors* are in evidence, particularly what Wilson identified as "the compactness of character and yet that feeling of roominess and space."[7] In fewer than twenty pages Adams takes the reader through two decades (1935–1955) in the lives of the Todds, during which time much happens to and within the family: Jessica sinks deeper into despair and dies—likely of a broken heart; Avery moves to San Francisco and marries twice, begins psychoanalysis, and has a serious love affair with a man in Hilton while married to her second husband; Tom has fallen in love with Barbara, a younger woman, during his marriage to Jessica, though he waits to marry her until after Jessica has died; Devlin has grown plump and sleek, has retreated into isolation from his job as a window designer at San Francisco's City of Paris department store after Jessica's death, has assigned blame for Jessica's death to Tom and Barbara, and, in the story's last section, has ironically established a warm relationship with Barbara after Tom's death, in the final section of the story; and Barbara in the end has returned to pause and reflect on her life after Tom's death, retreating to the Maine camp that first belonged to Jessica, where Barbara first met Tom.

By weaving the idea of "alternatives" through the story, Adams unites the strands of all these narratives spanning a three-decade period while maintaining a sense of "roominess and space." All of the characters (but especially Jessica, Avery, and Barbara) have committed their lives to—or thrown them away for—"some ideal of self." Jessica, most obviously, has committed herself to the pursuit of a romantic ideal, in one case evident in her romantic fantasies attached to Linton, that is utterly impossible in her life with Tom. She throws her life away in despair over her inability to realize her dreams. Barbara's idealism seems a bit less complex as it becomes clear that in her marriage to Tom she has achieved her ideal in assuming the socially constructed role that Avery designates as "something generic named Wife" (44). Avery is herself the one who anchors the concept of "alternatives": "But poor Avery was constantly plagued with alternatives; she constantly rewrote her life into new versions." (44). Avery, it seems, is searching for that self that will be realized only in unison with another person (that is, in romantic love, which again doesn't work out with her most recent Hilton lover). In this story she never finds it.

One of Adams's main points here, as well as in other stories and all the early novels, is that the different choices that people make in living their lives are not so much to be judged as they are to be accepted for what they are: alternative ways that individuals choose to live their lives, a point that allows the reader to have sympathy even for Tom, whose choices cause him mental anguish and depression. This point comes across in the story's final scene, which involves entering for a fleeting moment Barbara's consciousness as she reflects on her life and those others who have been part of it: "She sees all the people [Tom, Jessica, Avery, Devlin, her first husband], and herself among them, and for an instant she has a sense that she *is* all of them" (46). The moment of her epiphany is fleeting, and she immediately goes to work moving chairs and tables back to the way they were when she first came to the Maine cabin. She sheds some tears, but "she does not imagine an altered better life she might have had" (47)—a conclusion to the story that leaves open the question of whether Barbara has changed as a character by the end, though the point has clearly already been made that people make individual choices for reasons of their own and that work is important to one's survival regardless of the choices one has made.

The stories that cluster around the Todd stories in *Beautiful Girl,* related at least partly because of their shared North Carolina setting—and ultimately also because of shared characters, who will reappear in later stories, as well as closely related character types—are "Roses, Rhododendron," "Home Is Where," and, as noted earlier, "Beautiful Girl." "Roses, Rhododendron," one of Adams's finest and most lyrical stories set in a "sleeping village" in North Carolina that has features in common with the towns in the Hilton/Chapel Hill stories, shares more with the Todd stories than does any other Adams story. Similar to Adams's early novels, particularly *Families and Survivors,* "Roses, Rhododendron" explores the subject of friendship and the importance of it in the context of unhappy and broken families. The Avery character in "Roses, Rhododendron" is named Harriet Farr, and Adams uses a first-person narrator, Jane Kilgore, to tell the story of her "falling in love" many years ago—before she had a husband and children of her own—with the Farr family and with their house, which sat atop a hill, a mile outside the village in North Carolina to which Jane moved with her mother, Margot. It is on the gently sloping roof of the Farr house that Harriet and Jane, in that liminal space between childhood and adolescence, spend time together discussing their conceptions and misconceptions about sex. From their perch they can see "a yellow rosebush, rhododendron, a plum tree, and beyond [that] woods." The emotional effect of this view on Jane is "rich and careless, generous and somewhat mysterious" (206). The scene itself becomes a metaphor for the beauties of childhood innocence as seen against the complex and "somewhat mysterious" adult world, represented by the woods, that follows childhood.

Even in that past time of Jane's innocence there were hints of adult complexity, both in the Farr family and in her own. The Farrs on the surface, to Jane at least, are models of middle-class civility: they live in a beautiful house, are polite to each other, and have meals together. Only on one occasion at the dinner table do tensions come to the surface, revealing the deep conflicts that exist beneath the polite façade, and only later does Jane learn through her mother of rumors that Lawrence Farr had long ago fallen in love with a young, beautiful girl in town; though nothing came of their love, his betrayal of Emily clearly has left marks that account, at least partly, for the tension in the family. Jane also learns from Emily herself that she had dreams in her youth of becoming a writer, and now, as a wife who writes only book reviews and tends her flower gardens, she suffers deeply from the loss of those early dreams. Interestingly, Jane, whose father has left the family for a younger woman, has witnessed the broken dreams of her mother, who has had to establish a life without her husband. She now relies on a Ouija board to guide her in such major decisions as whether to move to North Carolina. The lives of the Farr family and the Kilgore family take the kinds of odd turns that adult life often brings: Margot reunites with Jane's father; they relocate to San Francisco and move forward with a life of ups and downs. Jane eventually graduates from Stanford, and she marries and has three children; Emily Farr leaves Lawrence, who develops emphysema; she moves to Washington, D.C., and then returns to care for him in the years before his early death. She dies shortly thereafter, and Harriet graduates from Radcliffe, going on to become a successful and well-known poet, marrying and divorcing twice. Eventually, through an exchange of letters, Jane and Harriet share memories of that time of childhood innocence before life had taken its many turns for both of them—life in a time when roses and rhododendron were in the foreground and the woods were visible off in the distance and "somewhat mysterious."

In "Home Is Where," the last North Carolina story in the volume, Adams uses the title to make a statement about the significance of the concept of home by begging a question with her title and offering at least a partial answer to an unstated theoretical question: where is one's home? And with that question and answer come others related to the connection of home to memory and of memory to dreams of youthful ideals that may have been lost in adulthood—questions and answers that resonate through many of the other stories in the volume, regardless of their setting. For Claire, the Avery-Harriet character in the story, home in a literal sense is "a small Southern river town, not far inland from the Atlantic coast" (153), though, in a later essay and from other details in the story, it is clear that Chapel Hill is the prototype for the town in "Home Is Where." Claire in the present time has returned with her son to this town where she grew up because, she says, "I needed to return to a place where I had been young." Her married life in San Francisco made her feel "ugly—drained and discolored, old," and in that condition, though married, she took a lover (154). Like Harriet and Avery, she is retreating from a complex adult world that she hopes to make sense of by coming home, though, also as for Avery and Harriet, the home of her childhood was a household in which there was barely suppressed hostility between her parents and a feeling of utter isolation for Claire. What she finds back home is a summer of love with a psychiatrist visiting from Boston, Dr. Caleb Jones, and their love affair gives back to her an ability to laugh and to see that there can be joy in life. The affair ends with the summer, her return to San Francisco, and her eventual loss of Caleb, who returns to his wife and family, but her summer at home has given her strength to divorce her husband and move forward as a stronger, more independent woman. Her return has allowed her to reconnect with the idea of home as containing the memory of laughter, joy, and innocence; that is a "home" she can carry with her everywhere thanks to that visit to the place of her youth. As she says at the end of the story, she "almost got used to being happy" (176).

The Hilton stories, like so many of Adams's stories, all involve her perspective on nostalgia and her view of the ways in which individuals use nostalgia to make sense of the past. In one of the very few scholarly articles on Adams's work, "Changing the Past: Alice Adams' Revisionary Nostalgia," Lee Upton carefully examines and categorizes how Adams's characters (and Adams herself) use the backward glance in ways that are sometimes destructive for the characters, as does Ardis Bascombe in what Upton characterizes as "static nostalgia," a limited use of nostalgia in which individuals refuse to accept the fact that the past exists unchanged in the present. Also destructive is the kind of nostalgia that Upton calls "vertiginous nostalgia," which characterizes the variety of nostalgia that Avery uses in "Alternatives": she envisions so many ways the past might have been altered that it creates in her something akin to vertigo. In other, more constructive instances individuals use nostalgia to gain strength to confront challenging situations, as Claire does in "Home Is Where" (34, 35–6). Claire's finding a summer love in the literal home of her past is a symbolic expression of her being able to find happiness in her present life back in San Francisco by drawing on the laughter and innocence that once existed alongside the less pleasant memories of home as she recalled it, an appropriation of the past that Upton characterizes as a positive use of "revisionary nostalgia."[8]

In the remaining stories in *Beautiful Girl* not discussed earlier, North Carolina does not play the role of home to any of the main characters, but in many of the stories there is a specific geographic location that functions in a similar way as the narrative moves forward and backward in time and laterally in geographical terms from San Francisco to a setting on the East Coast. In what is by almost any standard one of Adams's finest stories, "The Swastika on Our Door," Adams triangulates the setting, involving Virginia; Cambridge, Massachusetts (Harvard); and San Francisco, locales that appear in the three early novels. Little of the action in "Swastika" takes place in Virginia, but the southern background is central to the subjects of dreams, loss, lost causes, and ideas about home at the center of the story of these two brothers from Virginia, who first attend Harvard together and then take very different paths that provide the thematic binaries in the story. Skinny, sickly Richard tells Ellen, his companion, this about the small Virginia town of his youth, where conversations most often involved "the histories of other Southern families": the town was "a perfect background for eccentrics of the future." (91). At Harvard both brothers' eccentricities are obvious in their intentional caricaturing of privileged southern bigots, speaking loudly to each other as they read aloud in exaggerated southern accents from *Lee's Lieutenants* and tell racist jokes. When asked periodically by classmates in this present time of World War II if they don't know there is a war going on, both Richard and "fat Roger" are heard to respond, "Sir, the War has been over for almost a hundred years" (92). Such behavior during their Harvard years, which earns them the title of "Southern Fascists," results in their having someone chalk a black swastika on their door.

Those Harvard years are for Richard the happiest of times. However, they both graduate—Roger in economics and Richard in Greek—and Richard's bad heart forces him to retreat to Virginia to recuperate at home. He later returns alone to Harvard for a master's degree. Roger goes to San Francisco and becomes a successful lawyer and a social climber of the highest order. In an effort to reestablish the closeness with Roger he desperately wishes for, Richard finally follows Roger to San Francisco and takes a job teaching Greek, pursuing a life mainly in books and one in which he clings to chivalric ideals associated with the Old South. He has preferred to hold onto his inherited land and remain "land poor" rather than sell it and have more money than he needs. Roger, on the other hand, sold his inherited Virginia land quickly and gained from it much less than Richard makes later when he is forced to sell the land to make way for a Virginia highway, a sale from which he earns a fortune. Though Richard remembers the Harvard years as the best years of his life, they merit this status at least partly because they are anchored in the remembered years that Roger and Richard had growing up as brothers bound by their shared social marginalization—Richard by his illness, Roger by his "fatness"—as southern eccentrics in a small nameless town in Virginia. This Virginia town is Richard's "home," and nothing he tries can entice Roger to join him in recalling the days of their shared youth and their united championing—even if in parody—of the lost cause of the Confederacy. Roger, on the other hand, flourishes in San Francisco high society with no apparent nostalgia for the Virginia home of his youth or for his Harvard past; he finally marries Karen Erdman, daughter of wealthy German immigrants.

At a party at the Erdmans' house where Roger's engagement to Karen is to be announced, Richard, oblivious to the possibility he might offend many in his audience, raises this question to Roger in a voice loud enough to be heard by everyone: "Roger, remember the night they put the swastika on our door?" (103). And it is at this point that the reader begins to comprehend the dimensions of the tragedy that this story tells and the ways in which its losses are devastating to the characters that the reader has come to care most about: Richard and Ellen. After his question at the engagement party, Roger pushes Richard farther away, and only Richard's brilliant, beautiful, and mentally unstable companion Ellen is there to understand and lament his alienation from Roger. She is at Richard's deathbed, as is Roger, two months before the wedding, and she maintains a civil façade in Roger's presence. In the middle of the night hours after Richard's death, however, Ellen calls Roger and screams these words, among others: "pig pig pig pig! . . . You fat ugly murdering pig, you killed him with your never time to see him and your wall of fat German business friends always around you and your everything for a purpose and your filthy pig-minded greed and your all-American pig success and your so socially acceptable ambitions" (106). Years later Roger will explain much of this to his wife, who has found on his closet shelf a photograph of Ellen with Richard on the day he received $100,000 for the sale of his land. He tells her of Ellen's instability, which drove her into a mental hospital a few weeks after Richard's death, and suggests that her anger at him was likely over the fact that she was angry at not having received money from Richard's estate.

The reader knows that Roger is wrong and that he has likely lied to himself about Richard and about Ellen. The reader's dilemma, though, is this: how can one have so little sympathy for a successful San Francisco lawyer (Roger) who has, from all appearances, a happy marriage to a decent woman and several children that he both cares and provides for? And why would one have more sympathy for the brother who wants to affirm their bond of the past as southern spokesmen for the lost cause of the Confederacy and as tellers of racist jokes to their Harvard classmates (Richard)? Moreover, how can one view with sympathy a woman who rails so violently against a person who has, from all signs, done her no harm at all? There is, in fact, a bit of narrative magic involved here on Adams's part. Richard is emotionally and physically vulnerable: his heart disease renders him subject at any time to die, as he does at a young age; he is without shame or apology in his need for his brother's attention, which he had for so many years. He seems mainly to want Roger to acknowledge that they once shared that closeness—in other words, simply that they once shared a home that can be revisited in memory. There is no sign that Richard wishes to recreate the injustices of the Old South beyond superficially parodying them. He just wishes Roger to acknowledge that the two of them once had a home and that their love for each other existed. Roger has cast his lot with those in the present who can help advance him financially and socially, and there is no shred of evidence that he has any intention of owning a past—inhabiting a home in that past—that would perhaps place his present and future in jeopardy. He has, in essence, rejected his brother's plea for love, and the reader's sympathy for his neglect is difficult to come by.

It is easy, on the other hand, to find sympathy for Ellen, a brilliant mathematician whose insecurity may prevent her from accepting a full fellowship to Columbia. She becomes endearing to the reader because she is a person who is able to fully own the child she once was. With Richard at the duck pond in Golden Gate Park, she wades out in the water to be among the ducks, "like a child . . . [holding] her skirt out up in front of her" (96) and "out of the water, out of her element . . . a detached and languorous girl who sat . . . listening to [Richard's] tormented and violent Southern talk" (96). When Richard dies, Ellen feels his loss acutely, especially because she sees how easily a caring word from his brother could have made his life happier or even perhaps have extended it. Her scathing phone call to Roger in the middle of the night—which most readers are bound to agree with in substance—comes more from her heart than from her mental illness or her desire for money, as Roger would have Karen believe. As for Karen, Adams manages to show sympathy rather than disdain for her, much the way she shows sympathy for Barbara in "Alternatives": like Barbara, Karen simply cannot "imagine an altered, better life that she might have had" (47). With "The Swastika on Our Door" Adams presents the reader with a nuanced alternative way of thinking about love, loss, and the role of home in the lives of people who, once close, have gone separate ways. And she has done so with barely a hint of judgment.

In "What Should I Have Done?"—a story that raises questions about the duties of friendship—there is also a bicoastal element, and the story, which Adams will tell again in altered form in *Superior Women,* is the only one in *Beautiful Girl* in which the narrator is relentlessly judgmental. A native of Washington, D.C., the narrator considers herself southern, and during the early days of her close friendship with Maggie in "a good New England college" she brings Maggie home to meet "all the friends of my childhood, those nice Southern girls and boys." (222). Maggie, an Irish Catholic from Philadelphia, is not, the narrator notes in a nonjudgmental way, "pretty, by those exacting Forties standards," but the southern boys enjoy taking her on dates, though they finally "thought her 'fast' and didn't write [to her later], as otherwise they might have, inviting her to V.M.I. or Charlottesville" (223). Maggie and the narrator remain close after graduation, Maggie serving as maid of honor at the narrator's marriage ceremony; finally, after both wind up living "out West," Maggie confides to the narrator that she is pregnant. At first there is no judgment on the narrator's part, and as "a free-thinking protestant" she counsels an abortion, which Maggie as a Catholic cannot agree to. Years later, when the narrator is divorced and thinks herself pregnant by a married man, she seeks Maggie's companionship over dinner, at which time she learns that the father of Maggie's daughter was, in fact, a priest, a man that the narrator meets and speaks to briefly after Maggie's death some twenty years later. During those years the narrator has been caught up in complications in her own life and lost track of Maggie, only learning through a college magazine that she has died.

The thematic essence of the story is contained in the story's first and last scenes. It opens with a mention of the narrator's encountering Maggie's priest-lover at a dinner party after Maggie's death, an encounter that is "so upsetting that my breath tightens, my heart beats too fast, crazily, whenever I think of it, and I do think of it, obsessively. I wonder what I should have done" (221). The story ends with that rage-filled encounter, though one with no exchange of words, at a large dinner party with the priest—"Father Feeny—Richard, Dick" (229)—and with the narrator's thinking this to herself: "But I still wonder what, if anything, I should have done or said" (230). In highlighting the narrator's unspeakable ethical outrage in which Father Feeny is the villain, Adams leads the reader to question what an outsider can know about the details of anyone else's love for another person. By selectively omitting scenes that might have led the reader to understand more about Maggie's relationship with the priest, Adams invites the reader to interrogate alternatives to her vilification of Father Feeny and perhaps the complicity of Maggie, who found herself entangled in the mysteries of love. Also, the lack of details about what led to the narrator's withdrawal from Maggie's life challenges the reader to question the culpability of the narrator and to consider numerous plausible answers to her question of "What should I have done?" other than allow her friendship with Maggie to fall by the wayside, when Maggie at their last meeting was clearly in decline "in her old sweater, her hair dull and lank" (227). In the end Adams, in creating a severely judgmental narrator, prompts the reader to consider the psychological complexities involved in vilification, particularly when love is involved and when only part of the story is known.

In "A Jealous Husband" Adams uses a similar cross-country geographical setup to examine a particular variety of love relationship that rests less on idealization than on shared psychological need: the love between two southern eccentrics, Stuart and Martha Macmillan, both with high I.Q.s and "somewhat freakish looks." Stuart's "attachment" to Martha is seen as a chivalric act by people in their "medium-sized city in Virginia": "This was a very Southern and chauvinistic view [that] stemmed from a theory that such a fat girl was lucky to have a beau at all" and "ignored Stuart's equal (in conventional terms) unattractiveness" (110). The underpinnings of their relationship are psychologically complex, as this reference to Stuart's unattractiveness hints. In the end, his awareness of his vulnerability in this regard plays an important role in the evolution of his relationship with Martha. After marriage and their move to San Francisco, "their lives seemed to diverge" (112) as they shift back and forth in their roles of family breadwinners. The dynamics of their relationship appear to have been based originally on Stuart's "obsession" with Martha, an obsession that originated in her putdowns of him and her "putting down of his love" over dinners at a restaurant in their Virginia hometown. His obsession lessens after they marry and he begins to take her for granted.

It returns, however, as an "obsession with her infidelity" when Stuart discovers that Martha has had an affair with an African American colleague at the hospital where she is a medical secretary. Stuart comes to realize that as long as he can keep alive in his mind his "fantasies" of the details of her infidelities with her African American colleague, the passion in their relationship—sometimes expressed as sexual passion and at other times expressed through violence toward Martha—remains alive as long as they are together and married—in other words, as long as she is willing to accept him as her husband. What Stuart comes to realize by the end of the story is that his passion can be reignited over and over when "she [looks] like the mean old Martha who had sat across from him in the Porthole, at home, putting down his love" (123), an activity that Martha still seems to enjoy as she taunts him with remarks that keep alive the reality that she has engaged in an affair with another man. While there may have been unspoken, perhaps racial, underpinnings to their shifting levels of passion for each other, these remain at the level of the story's subtext. Stuart's regressive fantasies from the Virginia days of being accepted by Martha in spite of his unattractiveness remain in the foreground. Again, in this story Adams reminds the reader of the enduring presence of the past in everyone's life—in the centrality of those long-ago, "at home" years in the shaping of relationships in the present.

"A Pale and Perfectly Oval Moon" is one of Adams's most lyrical stories and her most probing examination of the power often exerted by an idealized love of the past to influence relationships in the present. The story is similar in many ways to "A Jealous Husband"—two of the three stories in *Beautiful Girl* in which the close, third-person omniscient viewpoint is focused on a male. Like "A Jealous Husband," the story is concerned with a relationship in which the husband, Val, is attempting to process his complex and puzzling feelings toward his wife, Penelope, a woman in the process of dying not so gracefully of an incurable illness. She incessantly taunts Val with comments about the types of women she knows he must be sleeping with during his time in San Francisco. He makes regular three-hour trips back and forth between their home in the high Sierras, where they have moved because it has seasons like those of Penelope's childhood New England home, to his lawyer's office in the city, on occasion remaining there overnight. In fact, Val is having an affair with Joan, a Kelly Girl who does temporary work from time to time in his office. Ironically, though, his thoughts about Penelope when he is with her are positive ones in which he recalls the beauty and complexity of the Penelope he fell in love with, glimmers of which he sees and thinks of in ways he does not share with her now. Ironic also is the fact that Val appears not to be attracted to the type of woman that Penelope insists on describing as his imagined lovers. Joan, for example, bears no resemblance to the "dark and sort of sleazy" women that Penelope fantasizes for him. From most indications, the pale and erudite Penelope was and remains his type: Joan has Penelope's coloring, notably the same color hair, which resembles Penelope's before she lost her hair during her illness.

After a brief remission, during which Penelope becomes again her cheerful, interesting former self, she dies, and Val marries Joan. Though Val and Joan's married life in San Francisco seems pleasant enough, even happy, Val begins to find her boring. Late at night when he finds himself up drinking alone since Joan typically goes to bed early, Val thinks of his past love for Penelope, both the lovable and the shrewish sides of her. In those moments he is able to say to her those things he was not able to say aloud when she was alive: "You're the most remarkable and interesting woman I've ever known. I've never really loved anyone but you" (188). On one level, Adams suggests with this facet of the story that fantasies can be and in fact often are preferable to reality. Allowing that Val's nostalgic fantasies regarding Penelope include both her good and her bad sides, these are still a function of memories over which Val has some control, and to some degree the Penelope of Val's mind is an idealized construction and subject to the vagaries of memory. Val can visit it at will without the intrusion of reality.

Running counter to this narrative, though, there is the hint of other loves in the lives of both Val and Penelope. For both of them there were apparently idealized loves in both of their pasts that remain hidden, loves that for both remain guiding stars. Val even believes that Penelope has somehow managed to go into remission on behalf of a "desperate love" in her past that he knows nothing of, and he himself had also "felt such desperation for his 'dark prize,' a feeling that he had forgotten, or that did not occur to him now" (186). His reference is to an idealized woman of his younger years that the reader learns he had loved, but their "acts of love" had been a disappointment (180). Perhaps the moon that Val sees on his way home to Penelope one night, a "ridiculously pale and perfectly oval moon, a perfect egg . . . a Humpty-Dumpty moon that disappeared behind a rock as quickly as, and foolishly as it had arisen," alludes to the brevity and paleness of Val's love for Penelope compared to the "idealized love" that seems to remain an unspoken presence in their relationships. The brief appearance of this moon and its fragility could, however, also refer to the suppressed memory—and possibly the persistence—of an idealized love. Adams leaves this image, which provides the story's title, open to interpretation, highlighting in the process her ever-present interest in the enduring mysteries and uncertainties of love, particularly that love that lingers from the distant past.

The other close third-person story in the volume told largely from a male's perspective is "Flights," which explores the sense of loss and loneliness that can result when one does not act on the impulse to share feelings of love toward another person. It is a story that closely resembles "A Jealous Husband" in that much of the story depends on what takes place in the mind of a married man, here Jacob Eisenman. Since the death of his parents, Jacob has been in retreat from the world, living on Kauai, "one of Hawaii's outermost and least populated islands" (125), in a vacation retreat of rental units and a bar that his parents had owned and cared for lovingly during the last years of their lives. Jacob maintains that he came to Kauai after their deaths; he remained there after he inherited the place because he fears flying and does not wish to make a return flight to Los Angeles, where he grew up. Now he is the unenthusiastic proprietor of a resort that is becoming shabbier by the season; he interacts very little with the resort guests and lives primarily in his books—among them volumes by Herman Melville and Jane Austen—shipped to him by his Berkeley landlady.

Jacob is effectively managing to withdraw into his own exclusive company, which he appears to prefer to the company of anyone he has met thus far. When Otto, his friend from college, comes with his wife, Joanne, for example, Jacob interacts with both of them only in a superficial way and winds up rejecting

Joanne's sexual advances when she slips into his room late one night, partly because he has concluded that she is "exceptionally stupid" (134). He resolves to tell his friend the next day that he is "married to a sub-moronic nymphomaniac" (136), but, of course, he does not because "for all Jacob knew Otto and Joanne were what is known as 'happily married'" (136). Such is what appears to the reader as Jacob's cynicism—though his evaluation of Joanne may actually in this case be more realistic than cynical—until his encounter and interaction with the beautiful and mysterious Valerie, which is the beginning of the relationship at the heart of the story.

From the moment Valerie arrives at the resort with Larry Cobb, her abusive husband or lover (it is never clear which), to stay for a week, it is obvious to Jacob that he and Valerie are connected in a deep way: early on, "Jacob understood that they were communicating on levels that he could not fathom" (132). In fact, they do clearly share some obvious qualities, such as a fear of flying, which both have for similar philosophical and psychological reasons and which they discuss at length. But they also have connections at a deeper level that are evident in his inferences about her past—about her marriages, about her long-ago wreck while in a convertible and the resulting scars on her face, and about the husband who died in the wreck—all correct intuitions on Jacob's part. And Valerie has similarly correct intuitions about Jacob—intuiting his hatred of the sun, for example. The things Adams manages so skillfully, however, are those "intuitions" of Jacob's that may or may not be correct but that create in him a sense of extraordinary intimacy with Valerie, which he is certain that she shares. He decides, for example, that she is not married to Larry, that her money is old money while Larry's is recently made, that there has been a knock on his door that has been made, he imagines, by Valerie.

The reader never learns if Jacob is right. The story effectively blurs the line between Jacob's imagination and reality in such a way that the reader is left with reasonable questions as to whether his connection with Valerie is a mystical one that could form the basis of a lasting relationship or whether it is largely a construction of Jacob's imagination. On the eve of her flight back to the United States, Valerie says this to Jacob: "God I may never get back on a plane." Jacob wishes at that moment to say, "Don't. Don't go anywhere, stay with me. Read all my books, and then I'll send for more. Talk to me when you want to. Stay" (138). He doesn't say this, though, and in the morning, as Valerie and Larry are about to leave, Jacob and Valerie "shook hands—their only touch" (140). In the end "Flights" is a story about Jacob's loss of what seems quite possibly to have been the love of his life, though he could not come out of his protective shell enough to discover if their love was real. The only certainty from the reader's point of view is that Jacob is left alone with an idealized image of Valerie, his books, and his dreams of what might have been, a situation similar to Val's and his desperation for his "dark prize" never won in "A Pale and Perfectly Oval Moon."

In the three stories discussed earlier—"The Swastika on Our Door," "A Pale and Perfectly Oval Moon," and "Flights"—the narrative focus is on males whose losses or anticipated losses are central thematic concerns: Richard loses Roger's brotherly caring; Roger loses Richard; Stuart loses Martha for a time to another lover; Val loses Penelope; Jacob loses Valerie. These losses involve an underlying, though usually unspoken, fear of abandonment or a mourning of the loss. Two stories in the volume—"Ripped Off" and "Attrition"—deal with similar kinds of losses from a female perspective. The fear of abandonment and the conscious recognition of loss come into the main characters' consciousness as something to mourn in both stories. In "Ripped Off" Deborah's first thought when she sees the contents of her desk drawer emptied on the bed is that Philip has abandoned her, not that she has been robbed. The consuming fear in her life is and has for a long time seemed to be, as her psychiatrist explained it to her, that "she feared abandonment. Her father had gone off to war and been killed . . . and it seemed (to the psychiatrist) that she tried to repeat that situation. She readily felt abandoned, and picked people who would abandon her" (80). The story does not finally attempt to assess the accuracy of such a psychological explanation for this primal human fear; rather, it presents fear of abandonment as one of the profoundly devastating feelings that often accompanies loss or the anticipation of loss. Even at the end of the day of the robbery, after she and Philip are safely and securely in bed for the night, Deborah cannot escape the haunting fear—expressed directly and indirectly by many of Adams's characters—that accompanies loss or anticipation of loss: "All her thoughts were unbearable, and she turned and pressed her body against the length of Philip's slender warm back, holding him tightly, as though she could keep him there" (86).

"Attrition" also addresses the subject of loss and anticipated loss directly, but from a different and more optimistic angle. It is not the loss of a lover that the narrator of "Attrition" is concerned with but rather the loss of close friends, Judith and Daniel X, who are moving from San Francisco to Israel. The narrator expresses her feelings about this in the first sentence: "I am taking it badly; I am in near-mourning over their imminent loss" (189). After cataloguing all of the reasons she will miss the Xs, the narrator begins to connect her dreaded loss of them to other losses in her life. The first is the relatively insignificant loss of a black purse—perhaps stolen, the narrator thinks; then she progresses to her understanding of her extreme reaction to such small things as the purse as an example of her general belief that "the world seems to me to be getting worse" (190). Finally she realizes that her "mourning" over the loss of the Xs is connected to her feelings about the deaths during the year of four people she knew well—five counting the death of her first husband's father. The narrator's ability to consciously link her relatively minor losses—the loss of her purse and then the loss of the Xs when they go to Israel, for example—allows her to understand her extreme reactions to losses of the moment: she is on some level becoming aware of and processing the most permanent of losses that come with mortality—with the human condition. Viewing loss through this lens allows the narrator to put the Xs' move to Israel in perspective, to ritualize it with a party, and to actually face anticipated loss with less desperation and even with a sense of hope that Deborah in "Ripped Off" has not yet been able to find.

The last three stories to be discussed in *Beautiful Girl*—"Winter Rain," "Gift of Grass," and "For Good"—form a trio whose central narratives revolve around the experiences of young women at the edge of adulthood who are about to enter (and are learning to deal with) a world of love affairs and the often baffling eccentricities of the "grown ups" who inhabit it—a world explored in many of the other stories in the collection. "Winter Rain," the very first story that Adams published commercially and one that immediately follows the Todd stories in *Beautiful Girl,* is told in flashback. It is set in Paris during the months following the graduation from college of Patience, the main character. She arrives in Paris—as Patience puts it, in that time of "Bennington meeting Princeton in the Montana Bar" (49)—and experiences for the first time not only another culture but also an idiosyncratic adult in that culture, Madame Frenaye, in whose house Patience takes a room. During that winter of 1947–1948 Patience also meets and falls in love with Bruno, an Italian young man who aspires to be a statesman and whom she finds exotic. Both Mme. Frenaye and Bruno make indelible impressions on Patience, as the painstakingly detailed account of Mme. Frenaye's house and meals and as Patience's descriptions of her intense meetings and partings with Bruno in Paris demonstrate. At one point after what seems to be one of many final partings from Bruno, Patience tells herself, "If I did not see Bruno again I would die" (58). Patience's overpriced room on the Rue de Courcelles in Mme. Frenaye's beautiful home provides the setting for Patience's improving her French, enjoying the exquisite meals prepared by Mme. Frenaye, and also realizing that Madame is gouging her by requiring such a high rent for a room in a house so far from her lectures at the Sorbonne and from Bruno. Patience and Madame finally part on less than friendly terms, later to have tea together at the Ritz and then in Patience's new room in the Latin Quarter on the Rue de Seine, both cordial meetings and the final one attended by both Bruno and Mme. Frenaye. Patience's last encounter with Mme. Frenaye at that final tea is formal, with no acknowledgment on Madame's part that any special bond had ever existed between them, though she had become a powerful presence in Patience's life in Paris. Patience's parting with Bruno is extremely painful, with Bruno informing her that she "would not be a suitable companion for an Italian statesman" (61).

Then, back in the United States, Patience appears from the moment she returns until the present, by which time she has a husband, kids, and a house, to minimize the importance of that extraordinary winter in Paris, "a crowded, wild, excited year" of her passionate love of Bruno and her intense bonding with Mme. Frenaye (49). And yet, oddly, she thinks of the indelibly imprinted memory of that winter in Paris that she has so vividly described only "whenever in the final unendurable weeks of winter, I am stricken as now, to the bone with cold—it is raining, the furnace has somehow failed." (49). The suggestion is that it takes a seemingly endless stretch of cold weather and rain in the present to trigger an association to those memories of the months of 1947–1948 in Paris. In those cold, rainy times she does indicate that it is Mme. Frenaye "of whom I think most often" (50).

The question that readers are bound to be puzzled by is why the Paris experience does not come into her mind or appear to cross her mind at other times of the year. In the present Patience has a husband, a house, and kids, and she sometimes (presumably only in those "unendurable weeks of winter") considers writing to Madame to send her pictures "to convince her that I have grown up, that I am no longer that odd girl who came to her in the wet summer coat, or who tried to charm her with tea made over Sterno in an unlikely room" (63). After the vivid description of her unforgettable winter in Paris, the question remains as to whether the adult Patience protests too much about rarely thinking of her Paris experience (and of never thinking of Bruno) in order to justify a compartmentalization of an important part of her life—perhaps even suppressing her memories until weather conditions make them inescapable. As she comments in the story's final sentence: "And I am forced to leave Madame, and Bruno of whom I never think, as and where they are, in that year of my own history" (62). Why is she forced, one wonders, to leave them there in memory to revisit only when there is a cold rain, and why does she maintain that she never thinks of Bruno, when obviously she does think of him? The story seems to hint that being a "grown up" in America—particularly being a grown-up woman in a male-centered society—may mean assuming a performative role and may well involve a partial denial or suppression of important parts of one's "own history."

Cathy, the main character in "Gift of Grass," the story immediately following "Winter Rain" in *Beautiful Girl* and the first Alice Adams story published by the *New Yorker,* is a bit younger than Patience was during her winter in Paris, and she is in open rebellion against the role of wife, mother, and homemaker that Patience eventually takes on. She asks her psychiatrist, with whom she has a combative relationship, "But what's so great about money—or marriages and houses, for that matter?" (65). She has told her mother and her stepfather, Barbara and Bill, that she "was not going back to school in the fall," which has prompted Barbara, with the best of intentions, to declare her "troubled," set her up with regular appointments with her own psychiatrist (and Bill's), and express the hope that Cathy will plan to get married, apparently under the assumption that she is pregnant. Cathy "lie[s]" that she is not troubled and truthfully says that she has no plans to get married. She simply "[doesn't] want to go to school for a while" (66). In her therapy session with Dr. James Fredericks, Cathy is resistant to his urgings to tell him about her likes and dislikes. She calls him a "dumb fink" (67), and Dr. Fredericks admits to himself that he dislikes Cathy, as he struggles with his countertransference. Then, because of his knowledge of Bill's connection to hunting, gleaned from his therapy sessions with Bill, Dr. Fredericks finally manages to get Cathy to admit to her hatred of deer hunters.

The story ultimately turns on this subject of deer hunters when later in the evening, at dinner, Cathy confesses to Bill and Barbara that she had told Dr. Frederick about her hatred of deer hunters, an admission that brings out in Bill after his second drink a revelation that he also detests deer hunters because his father was a deer hunter. "To tell you the truth," Bill says to Cathy and Barbara, "I was afraid of him. The way I find hunters frightening" (72). After Barbara has gone upstairs with a headache, Cathy and Bill are alone cleaning up the dishes, and Bill says what he has wanted to say to Cathy for quite some time: "You think you're confused, and that the world is difficult. Christ, what do you think it's like to be forty-one? Christ, talk about confused and difficult" (74–75). This obviously becomes a breakthrough moment for Cathy, who quietly before she goes up to bed leaves two marijuana joints in the middle of Bill's desk on a white sheet of paper. When he finds them, his eyes sting with tears and he falls asleep in his chair.

Like many adolescents in Adams's fiction who are about to enter the adult world, Cathy has been confused by the seeming hypocrisies that she has witnessed in those in her life who are performing grown-up roles. Her twice-married mother, who "was an extremely nice woman who wanted things to be perfect—her house, her husband, her daughter and especially herself" (72)—quite often pretends that they *are* perfect, even as she lamely attempts to conceal the fact that she is sending Cathy to her psychiatrist. Only Bill, who is "exceptionally sensitive to the feelings of women" (71), is willing to break through the adult persona of hypocrisy and admit that he, too, often feels the confusion that Cathy is feeling, and he is able to tell her in detail about some of the difficulties of adult life. "Being married is a hell of a lot more difficult than not being married, let me tell you," he says to her. "And it's very hard to live without a lot of money and booze. You give it a little thought—just try." This is honesty that Cathy has apparently not seen before in an adult, and it helps her bridge the space between her adolescent world and the adult one. She does accept Bill's challenge and obviously "give[s] it a little thought": On one hand, she shows she is able to empathize with Bill in his pain and to symbolically extend herself across generations with her "gift of grass"—self-medication, other than Bill's usual alcohol, that has worked for her and may, she hopes, work for him; on the other, she also acknowledges in the process that she appreciates the honest snapshot into the difficulties of the adult world she is about to enter.

Adams concludes *Beautiful Girl* with "For Good," whose events are seen largely through the eyes of a keenly observant twelve-year-old girl, Nell Ashbury. The story opens with a party that provides a microcosmic view of a world in which the endless confusions in relationships she sees around her have influenced Nell's decision never to marry. In this world, however, there are glimmers of hope that, from all indications, will allow Nell to survive into adulthood with her idealistic spirit intact. The most surprising source of Nell's hope comes oddly from Pauline Field, a once-productive and well-known abstract-expressionist painter, who is hosting the party Nell is attending with her father, Jason, and her trim, blond stepmother. Though Pauline is not attractive—"a huge strong woman, dressed outrageously in pink" and with "wild white hair and consuming dark-brown eyes"—Nell is immediately fascinated by her, and in spite of the fact that Pauline is crying out to her guests, "How I hate California!" (231), Nell perceives her as someone she should listen to. This is due to the fact that Pauline is, to Nell, "more *present* than anyone else there" and also because "Pauline listens." In this regard she is different from the friends of Nell's mother, with whom she lives on the East Coast—those "grownups (her mother's writers) [who] ask questions and then don't wait to hear the answer." Nell is tired of "literary people, who all talk too much" (232).

Nell's interest in and liking of Pauline is ironic. She has been taught by her thin mother to be leery of "fat women" because "women who hate their husbands always put on weight" (233). It is perhaps also ironic that Nell is so close to her father, with whom she doesn't live and who is technically one of those "literary people" Nell is ostensibly tired of, though her father does not appear to be one who talks too much. He is a frustrated writer who had one very successful novel many years ago but who has been unable to write another book since then. He is, however, one of the other reasons Nell sees a glimmer of hope in the adult world. She looks like him; they confide in each other (most recently, on the day of the party, he has told her that he has at last begun a new novel); and "she trusts his skill at the wheel," clearly symbolic of her trust in the honesty and goodness in her father (239).

Also, she senses a special connection between Pauline and Jason, partly because she and her father seem to be almost the only two at the party who actually listen to Pauline when she talks. When Pauline invites Nell to join her in the kitchen to help get the food ready to serve, the two form a bond, based partly on Pauline's insights into her father's years-long writer's block and the belief of both that "the really important thing is never to marry" (237). Their bond causes Nell to worry when Pauline drunkenly leaves her own party and her guests on foot and wanders off alone. Others at the party do not seem concerned, though Nell sees apparent in her father's face "her own feelings. . . . Jason looks stricken, deeply shocked, as she is. . . . Will she plunge drunkenly into that cold bleak ocean, that terrible Pacific?" (239). Both she and Jason are aware of the fact that each could lose something precious.

Nell from the beginning has intuitively known all along that there is something permanent—perhaps love, which Nell yet knows very little about personally—between Pauline and her father: "Did Pauline once love her father? Did they have an affair back in the Forties?" (237). Nell's mother will tell her a month later that they did. All along, Nell has been looking for something solid that she can count on in this life of adults who, for the most part, do not listen and do not say what they mean. Early in the story, when Pauline is crying out that she hates California, Nell takes her at her word, as she does at that age tend to believe "that what is said is meant, for good" (232). When later, on a beach in Ipswich, Massachusetts, Nell's mother tells her that she has learned in a letter from Jason that Pauline has left her third husband, Stephen, and "gone off to San Miguel de Allende to study painting there" (241), Nell is "glad" and digests the news as "something deeply known or felt before." Without any further knowledge as to whether Jason plans to leave his wife and join Pauline but knowing that both are back at work painting and writing, Nell imagines "Jason and Pauline (a Pauline brown and thin, renewed) on a bright hot windless tropical beach. For good" (242). It is an affirmation of the plight of the romantic idealist—in this case a young and still rather innocent one—in a world in which there are on all fronts the risk of loss and the danger of self-deception—the world that is explored from many angles in the "banquet of riches" of *Beautiful Girl*.

A common thread that unites the stories in *Beautiful Girl* is the subject of relationships—of connections between people—that are anchored in forces that bring individuals together in hopeful moments and often break them apart, leaving them sometimes with unspeakable sadness and regret: there are love relationships that are based often on romantic idealization, like Greene's love for Ardis in "Beautiful Girl" (closely akin to Daisy's in *Careless Love*), which often leads to feelings of loss and disillusionment; there are loves that are freeing, like Verlie's for Horace, and that lead to happiness and peace, at least for a time (similar to Eliza's for Harry in *Listening to Billie*); there are friendships with love, like Jane's love for Harriet in "Roses, Rhododendron" (similar to Louisa's attachment to her childhood friend Kate in *Families and Survivors*); and there are loves, like Richard's for Roger and Richard's for Ellen in "The Swastika on Our Door," that lead to heartbreak (akin to Eliza's love for Evan and then for Reed in *Listening to Billie*). In *Beautiful Girl*, Adams powerfully authenticates Beverly Lowry's often-repeated observation that "NOBODY writes better about falling in love than Alice Adams."[9] But Adams also demonstrates in this collection an ability to explore many varieties of the unspeakable sadness that often comes in the wake of love that once existed but now has been lost.

CHAPTER 4

1980s Novels

Rich Rewards, Superior Women, and *Second Chances*

Rich Rewards (1980)

Coming one year after *Beautiful Girl* and two years after Adams's previous novel, *Listening to Billie, Rich Rewards* is a pivotal work. It is Adams's only novel written from the first-person point of view, and in Daphne Matthiessen Adams creates what Larry Blades characterizes as Adams's "ideal of the contemporary woman."[1] Daphne shares much in common with the main female characters of the first three novels and many of the stories. However, unlike Daisy in *Careless Love,* Louisa in *Families and Survivors,* Eliza in *Listening to Billie,* and all of those whose narratives are told through the filter of an omniscient author/narrator who guides the reader through the journeys of the main characters with sometimes-godlike insights and knowing parenthetical observations, Daphne tells her own story, revealing at each turn the insights that allow her to move from one stage of her development to the next. Much of the power of *Rich Rewards* rests in Daphne's progressive understanding of the steps that lead her finally from a position of relative weakness and vulnerability to one of strength and autonomy.

In the novel's first few pages Daphne grounds her story in three details that mark her first week in San Francisco, where she is decorating the house of Agatha Marshall, her closest friend from boarding school and now a doctor in "that spoiled and lovely city" (3). The first two details—the theft of her garbage can and the random murder of a man out for a walk in the neighborhood with his dog—will figure finally into the broader social and political dimensions of Daphne's story. The third is her discovery that Jean-Paul, a former lover she met in Paris while on her honeymoon twenty years ago, will soon be coming to the San Francisco area. By the end of the first chapter Daphne has introduced the subjects that will provide the basis for the most important themes of the novel: choice (the decision to leave a bad relationship), chance or coincidence (an opportunity that provides the impetus to separate oneself from a relationship geographically), work (an authentic, constructive reason to change locations), love (the possibility of an old love that may have survived), theft (a symptom of a breakdown in the natural order—the threat of chaos), and violence (murder that takes place randomly and afflicts the innocent). The tidiness of the arrangement of the novel's thematic foundation in the first chapter will become clear by the end of the novel.

On the most superficial level of Daphne's narrative the tension derives from the romantic/realist binary at work throughout the novel. From the first mention of Jean-Paul's scheduled lectures at Berkeley, the reader wonders (as does Daphne) whether a once-passionate love from one's youth like that between Jean-Paul and Daphne could possibly have survived twenty years of neglect. As Daphne recalls, even back during the high point of their passion for each other, "quite possibly Jean-Paul, a realist, knew all along that I was just a big sexy American girl about whom he felt very intensely for a while" (14). The question of what will come of the inevitable meeting between Daphne—clearly an accomplished, intelligent woman, albeit one with a persistent romantic-idealist streak—and Jean-Paul, at least once a realist, provides much of the tension of the novel. From beginning to end, Daphne, who believes Jean-Paul has been the love of her life, anticipates how she will arrange to see Jean-Paul, how he will appear to her as a fifty-year-old man, and how she will appear to him as a forty-year-old woman. When they finally do meet in the penultimate chapter, stand there "kissing, like people famished for love" (197), go on to spend several blissful weeks together, and plan to go back to France for a life together, some readers might conclude that romance has triumphed—in the end a debatable conclusion.

The majority of the novel's reviews were positive, but, not surprisingly, some reviewers found the seemingly happy, romantic ending contrived, and they complained about the many seeming coincidences in the novel. Adams responded to this line of criticism by saying, "I thought I had written a political novel but the reviewers think it is romantic."[2] She was, no doubt, well aware of the fact that *Rich Rewards* contains a complex mixture of the romantic and the political, and on one level its multiple "happy endings" are clearly to be read as ironic. For all of the superficial happiness and optimism in the reunion of Daphne and Jean-Paul, for example, there is an undercurrent of reservation in Daphne's voice as she thinks about their future. They are not, after all, the young, romantic heroine and hero of twenty years ago about to embark freshly on the adventure of life. Jean-Paul is suffering from advanced emphysema, one of the risks to their future happiness that concerns Daphne enough to discuss it with Agatha. She also sees another possibility: "Suppose, in a long-run day-to-day way, we just didn't get along too well?" (205). Even the mood of Daphne's verbs in describing their projected life together in Paris shifts to the conditional as their romantic "vacation" together comes into its last week, close to the time they would leave together for Paris: "By then I would have finished Agatha's house, and Stacy's. Agatha and Royce could move into their house as Jean-Paul and I moved out. We would cross the country and then the Atlantic" (203). Then, in the last sentence of the book, Daphne adds, "In any case, that's our plan," an open-ended statement that suggests at least some uncertainty as to whether the plan will work out (205).

There is uncertainty as well in all of the other happy endings of the novel. It seems unlikely that Derek, Daphne's pathologically cruel lover from Boston, will live happily ever after with his newfound love, with whose name he has malevolently taunted Daphne. And Daphne implies that there is some question as to whether Royce will get sober and become a faithful husband to Ruth, given his increasing reliance on alcohol and his history of infidelity. Already Daphne has seen his self-destructive influence infect Agatha, who has become uncharacteristically anxiety-ridden and, as evidence of Royce's negative influence on her, has begun smoking again. It would seem that the old, decadent order that Daphne has witnessed and described realistically in so many pages of the novel has prevailed in the end. Even the mysterious and seemingly ill-gotten money from Agatha's father, the General—and the unearned fortunes of those like Stacy, Royce's former mistress—continues to fuel the decadent lifestyles lived by those who surround Daphne. The reader is left, in effect, with the suggestion that the happy endings in the novel are tentative at best. They rely on unlikely coincidences and on the foundation of an old order represented by the General's money, presumably obtained unlawfully and through acts of violence.

It is here that the political and romantic aspects of the novel intersect, and the reader is likely to recall the three details that confronted Daphne during her first week of work on Agatha's house in San Francisco, "that spoiled and lovely city": the theft of her garbage can, the murder of a man in the neighborhood out walking his dog, and the publicized arrival in the area of Jean-Paul. The last of these details points to the coincidence, contrivance, idealization, and fantasy—the romance—that is woven, finally with ironic effect, into the fabric of the novel. The theft of the garbage can and the murder foreshadow the lawlessness, violence, and chaos everywhere present in Daphne's everyday life in the "spoiled and lovely city," itself a microcosm of the world of the 1970s.

Shortly after the garbage can theft, Daphne returns to find her house has been robbed, and the robber, with a "snobbishly selective eye," has taken her finest clothes—silk blouses, cashmere sweaters, her most expensive scarves and dresses—leaving behind the cheaper things. The robber has even neatly stacked her mail on the hall table. The lawlessness has moved from outside with the garbage can theft to inside, and Daphne naturally feels "nakedly exposed to an unknown, hostile person" (54). The hostility is earlier foreshadowed in a visit from Whitey Houston, who would, as it turns out, act out his anger in his brutal beating of his sister Caroline. Whitey himself would later be murdered during a violent confrontation after he has moved to Alaska. Daphne appears to see in the end (as Adams has seen from the beginning) that this lawlessness and violence are an outward manifestation of the moral vacuum and rudderless drifting toward meaningless reward—the chaos—of contemporary society,[3] which has become a contemporary representation of T. S. Eliot's wasteland.

There are indirect allusions to Eliot's *The Waste Land* throughout *Rich Rewards,* among them a reference late in the novel to April ("the cruelest month" from the first line of Eliot's poem), which Daphne describes in this way: "April, that year in San Francisco, was cold and wet" (178). Appropriately following the cold and wet time of "the cruelest month" come Agatha's calls revealing that Ruth, Royce's wife, has disappeared and is soon to get a divorce from Royce in Puerto Rico; that Royce is drinking more and more; and that Tony, Daphne's beautiful and beloved carpenter, has been jailed for male prostitution. Then there is a festival-celebration for Agatha and Royce's wedding on "the most beautiful day [Daphne has] ever seen in California, a pure blue and golden day"—one of those rare days when there is no news of plane crashes or accidents, a day when "there [seems] to be a suspension of calamities" (189). Beautiful as the day seems, Daphne makes it clear to the reader that such beauty is likely ephemeral, particularly given what she knows about the particulars of Royce and Ruth's relationship.

After the wedding Daphne and Jean-Paul have a blissful reunion, and they spend one week in Royce's cabin on Lake Tahoe as fall approaches. Daphne makes the following observation about their week together there: "Everywhere you looked the scene said summer, all the blue green gold day, and although you desperately wanted to believe that it was summer, and that the summer would last forever, still you knew—you couldn't not know, that autumn was fairly close at hand. I would, at that time, have given anything in the world for time to go back just one week, to let us start our week up there over again. But soon it would be September, then October; and often in November the snows begin around there" (204). The language here, coupled with the qualifications and reservations Daphne has already expressed about the likelihood of a sustained relationship with Jean-Paul, suggests that Daphne has absorbed a central lesson of her year in San Francisco: she has come to understand that endings are happy only in a qualified way and often, as is true of most of the happy endings in the novel, happy in quite an ironic sense. She wonders this aloud to Jean-Paul: "Why did I happen to become so involved in the violent downfall of that family? What did it mean, my year in California?" (203). He dismisses the importance simply as an accident. That, he says, "is how history occurs" (203).

Later Daphne will partly agree, though she has never believed entirely in accidents and though "it seemed to [her] that all the year had been leading to this one enchanted week with Jean-Paul" (203)—a time that seems unlikely to have a future beyond the moment and a time, perhaps, to be savored only in its moment. Even as she fantasizes about what her life might be like with Jean-Paul, she comes back to another true lesson of her year in San Francisco. Her work is the thing that gives her life direction and purpose: "I planned to study furniture design in a serious way. What with the various uncertainties involved in our plan, including Jean-Paul's health, I had, at last, to concentrate on work" (204). Daphne is prepared finally to ground her life in her occupation, and in this regard she is soon to be followed by Megan Greene—also to become Adams's ideal of the contemporary woman—who rises to the top of her profession as a literary agent in Adams's next novel, *Superior Women*.

Superior Women (1984)

Adams had published four novels and two collections of short stories when *Superior Women* appeared, in 1984. Her novels, with the exception of *Careless Love*, had received generally positive reviews, and her story collections had been favorably reviewed and praised. Her stories had been appearing regularly in the *New Yorker* since 1969, and from the beginning she had begun to develop, according to one reviewer, a devoted following, particularly among the literary elite.[4] One reviewer predicted that after *Superior Women* "the elitism [would] vanish" and that the novel would "put Alice Adams on the map,"[5] as, indeed, it did, remaining to this day the best-known Alice Adams work. *Superior Women* rose quickly to number one on the *San Francisco Chronicle* list of best sellers and to number twelve on the *New York Times Book Review* best-seller list. It also earned Adams more than a half-million dollars from the sale of paperback rights to Ballantine—this in addition to a sizable advance against royalties from Knopf. Becoming a best-selling author, of course, brought increased scrutiny from reviewers, as the large number of reviews that came in the wake of her novel's publication demonstrates. The reviews were, on balance, positive, but the negative ones—and some of them were brutal—typically pointed to those qualities of *Superior Women* that, in the reviewers' opinions, gave the novel its best-seller qualities: its characters were stereotypes; its insights, banal; its scenes, contrived and soap operatic. A majority of the reviewers, however, granted that Adams knew what she was doing artistically and that she was using stylistic devices in subtle and skillful ways.

Adams stated that when she first began writing *Superior Women* she intended to write "an unofficial history of the years I know about, the 40s to the present."[6] And she planned to have an outline: "I had a fantasy of oversized paper and lists and dates. It was going to be wonderfully neat and coordinated. I think I was thinking of some of F. Scott Fitzgerald's outlines and notebooks. But I never did that."[7] What she did, perhaps inadvertently, was create a character-driven novel with a main female character, Megan Greene, who finds herself in the plight of a Fitzgerald hero at the beginning of the novel. Megan is an outsider looking in—a status reminiscent of many of Fitzgerald's characters as well as of Fitzgerald himself. She is a Californian from Palo Alto working in a Stanford bookstore when she becomes enchanted with the eastern United States after her summer romance with George Wharton, a proper New Englander. George will go back to medical school in Boston at the end of the summer of 1942, but by then Megan's imagination, like Jay Gatsby's or Nick Carraway's, has been captured by her visions of the sophisticated East. She applies and is accepted to Radcliffe, and there she meets the three other "superior women"—Lavinia Harcourt, Peg Harding, and Cathy Barnes—who become her friends and are at the heart of the novel from the beginning.

Of the four, Megan qualifies as the most naïve regarding knowledge of the subtle class distinctions and conventions of the Northeast, and although Adams chooses an omniscient point of view for the novel, shifting the focus of narration among the four main characters, Megan clearly is the central character, evolving over the course of the novel into what, as one reviewer put it, "some readers now regard as 'the Alice Adams woman'—bright, honest, attractive, thoughtful—and sometimes a bit offbeat."[8]

Megan's development provides a strong unifying thread in the novel, as the development of her character into a strong Adams heroine fuels the forward motion of the narrative across four decades. From her first encounter with George in the early pages of the novel, Megan displays a brightness that comes through in their interactions, though the verbal exchanges are brief and marked more by necking than by talking. Her intellectual ability is confirmed by her acceptance to Radcliffe and then by her graduating summa cum laude in three years. She goes on to distinguish herself in her profession, working first at a publishing house in New York and then as a partner to a very successful literary agent, an association that brings Megan much prestige and money. It also enhances her self-esteem. Her increasing attractiveness is also something that Adams develops subtly over the course of the novel, and it is associated with her increasing sense of self-worth, her changing taste in clothes, and her enduring attention to her weight and body image. As she becomes more successful in her work, Megan becomes increasingly thin, stylish, and self-confident—all qualities associated with Adams's most admirable female characters and qualities that Lavinia notices each time they meet after years of not seeing each other. George Wharton also notices Megan's transformation when they meet again more than fifteen years after their first encounter in the Stanford bookstore. He is now a doctor, he is divorced, and his life has taken a downward turn, while Megan has become so attractive that she is almost unrecognizable to him. George is so burdened by his own problems at the time of their meeting that he doesn't realize that part of the attractiveness of the "new" Megan comes from the fact that she is extremely kind and welcoming to him, a quality that Adams attributes in large part to Megan's having found fulfillment in her work. And finally, true to her role as "the Alice Adams woman," Megan is "a bit offbeat," evidenced by her unwillingness to behave in certain ways simply because they are socially acceptable. One among numerous examples is her affair with Jackson Clay, an African American trombone player, during a time when interracial dating was considered socially unacceptable, especially by her racist friend Lavinia.

Throughout the novel Adams contrasts Megan's character and the stages of her individuation with Lavinia's, throwing into relief the generally destructive direction Lavinia's self-centeredness takes year by year. It seems no accident that, of the two, Lavinia is the one who has at no time over the four decades of the novel involved herself in work. When Lavinia and Megan first meet, Lavinia is, in the words of one reviewer, "a golden girl in the tradition of F. Scott Fitzgerald's heroines,"[9] and Megan is puzzled that Lavinia would seek out her friendship because they have very little in common. They are, as Megan imagines it, "tall thin blond, impeccably expensively dressed Lavinia" and "plump dark Megan, in her slightly wrong California clothes" (18). Lavinia is a Washington, D.C., debutante who attended a southern boarding school, at which she was the brightest and most sophisticated student. Her parents own a lavish Washington home and a country house in Fredericksburg, Virginia. She is universally sought after for dates, and her female classmates wish simply to be associated with her. Megan is understandably puzzled that Lavinia would have chosen not only her but also the overweight Peg and the not especially attractive Cathy for friends; however, she finally concludes it is because she

(Megan), Peg, and Cathy are all very bright and thus serve as an appreciative audience for Lavinia's razor-sharp wit.

As the novel moves across the four decades, Adams uses the omniscient viewpoint to allow the reader to view the contrast by observing Megan's treatment of Peg and Cathy and to compare it to Lavinia's. During their first year in college Lavinia is at least on the surface kind to Peg, who is supposedly her best friend, and offers only superficial and occasional good-natured comments about her weight. After Peg becomes pregnant, marries Cameron Sinclair, and moves to Texas, Lavinia becomes judgmental and is snide in her remarks to others about Peg. As she writes Megan, "Well the most interesting news from our little Peglet: she's pregnant. I can just see her with a whole family of great big children, can't you? And she will get bigger and bigger" (103). When she later visits Peg, she appears to be gracious in helping her prepare a meal for guests when Peg's cook is too ill to come to work, but she does it in a way that demonstrates her own competency at Peg's expense. During the visit she mocks Peg's growing commitment to civil rights, a cause that Peg comes to embrace so fully that it leads to her freedom from the conventional life and the confining gender role to which she has been bound throughout her marriage.

By contrast, Megan becomes a beacon of hope to Peg, and in her darkest emotional times she writes letters to Megan in which she confides her deepest fears. One of these desperate letters concludes, "I am afraid. I do everything wrong" (154). But Peg never mails the letters. They reach only Cameron, who finds them and rightly understands them to be evidence of Peg's desperate emotional state. In a telephone call, Lavinia tells Megan that Peg has had an emotional breakdown and even absurdly implies that Megan is somehow partly to blame for not having paid more attention to Peg. Lavinia does, however, visit Peg after her breakdown, and generous-hearted Peg credits her with loyalty, though she does wonder much later if Lavinia's politeness has perhaps always concealed some less honorable qualities. In the end, after Peg recovers, acknowledges her need to devote her energies to furthering the cause of civil rights, buys a farmhouse in Georgia and establishes it as a safe house for people escaping oppression, and openly acknowledges her love for a woman who is also a civil rights worker, Megan and Peg become "good trusted, and trusting friends" (280). Through her contrasting of Megan and Lavinia, Adams explores her increasing interest in her fiction in the dynamics of friendship. In the process she also hints at the decreasing necessity for a woman to predicate her success on the constant presence of a man in her life.

The novel concludes with an epilogue that takes place at Peg's Georgia farmhouse in June 1983, four decades after the freshman year during which Megan, Lavinia, Peg, and Cathy first met. And here Adams brings together many of the ideas she has explored in the novel: the value of work in an individual's self-esteem; the importance of friendship and of family; the need for resilience in an often chaotic and hostile world. Some ten years before these final scenes of the epilogue, Cathy has died of cancer; and a few years after her death Lavinia and her husband, Potter, have celebrated thirty years of marriage in a relationship that has apparently been without love. Megan, now a very successful agent in her mid-fifties, has been able to rescue her mother, Florence, from her state of abandonment by Megan's father; and she is able to do this because her work has given her the resources, both financial and emotional.

The characters in the epilogue have all lived through decades of social and political change; World War II, the civil rights movement, Nixon's presidency and Watergate, the Vietnam War, and the feminist movement of the 1960s and 1970s have affected them all to varying degrees. In the present—June 1983—with Cathy dead and Lavinia in her bubble of superiority, only Peg and Megan of the original four friends can attend Florence's birthday celebration. Though they all think of the house as Peg's, it is now actually co-owned by Peg, Vera (Peg's partner), Megan, and Florence, and it serves as "a temporary shelter, a way-station hospitality house for the homeless, mostly women but sometimes men too" (358). The four co-owners are joined in joyful celebration by Henry Stuyvesant (a former lover of Megan and Lavinia), Jackson Clay (Megan's African American lover), Biff Malone (Megan's gay former coworker), and Rex Sinclair (Peg's displaced and rudderless son).

Some reviewers found it implausible that so many of the novel's main characters would be able to come together in the epilogue in a scene of celebration and harmony. It is in this ending, however, that Adams bridges the gap between the social realism of her "informal history of the 40s to the present" and her deeply ingrained romanticism. From a realistic perspective it is certainly plausible and a cause for celebration that all the individuals, many of whose lives have been intricately connected throughout the novel, choose and are able to come together to celebrate a birthday. The reader has come to know each of these characters—different as they are from one another in age, race, sexual orientation, and gender—enough to understand the logic of their consciously electing to be there. But present here also is Adams's romanticism in what Carolyn See characterizes as *Superior Women*'s "Utopian ending": "Its goodness and optimism seem at first as hard to believe as Lavinia's wicked energy. But when you think about this improbable reconciliation between sexes and generations you see that it can be true."[10] The novel's powerful coda—its epilogue—juxtaposes the possibility that there can be a world of peace and harmony as it exists in Peg's house against the knowledge that outside the connectedness of that safe house there is a world that, in one reviewer's words, contains "the disconnections of contemporary life."[11] Both of these are worlds Adams has explored before and would soon venture into again in *Second Chances.*

Second Chances (1988)

Second Chances, set in the small town of San Sebastian, California, south of San Francisco, deals with an enclave of affluent, intelligent, thoughtful, and highly mannered friends that one member of the group describes as "almost *old* . . . a party of nearly old people." This character goes on to say, "We are the sort of people I used to look at and wonder why they even bothered getting so dressed up" (84). Though several minor characters on the novel's periphery play important roles, these six friends come into the sharpest focus in the novel: Dudley Venable (a journalist and perhaps the closest thing to the novel's central character) and her husband, Sam (a painter); Celeste Timberlake (a widow who has just lost her husband); Edward Crane (a published poet in an earlier time, though now a rarely working realtor), who lives with his younger lover of thirty years, Fernando ("Freddy") Fuentes, a professor of Spanish and Portuguese; and Polly Blake (a wealthy, free-spirited eccentric and a cancer survivor), who pursues an active relationship with a lover, taking a trip to Europe with him near the end of the novel. All of these friends (except Freddy), who are on the threshold of "old age" and past their prime career-wise, range in age from the mid-sixties to seventy, the age of Edward.

More than in any of her previous fiction, Adams in *Second Chances* is interested in the subject of friendship, which, while it is to a lesser degree a theme in all of her earlier novels, is at the center of *Second Chances.* Most of the friendships in *Second Chances* have existed for three or four decades, similar to the length of the friendships in *Superior Women.* However, all of the friendships in *Second Chances* have unique origins, none of them resembling the college-classmate friendships of Megan, Lavinia, Peg, and Cathy in *Superior Women.* Adams is concerned in *Second Chances* with the dynamics of friendships among those who have lived in proximity to one another for a decade or so, during which time each person has confronted the specter of old age and his or her own mortality while others close by are doing the same.

To explore friendship from this angle, Adams constructs characters in *Second Chances* who are approximately a decade older than those in *Superior Women,* at the end of which the four friends are just passing their mid-fifties. *Second Chances* is a departure from the "typical" Alice Adams novels that have preceded it, novels in which the central figures have usually been younger, quite vital, and characteristically sexually active; understandably, Adams was asked repeatedly in interviews following publication of the novel why she, at the age of sixty-one, had chosen to write a novel about old age. In one interview she responded in this way: "I am almost old. I'm 61, and as I look ahead, I wonder what it will be like. And a few years ago, I became involved with a group of older people, and I got interested in their lives."[12] In another interview she brought in an even more personal dimension related to her own fears concerning aging and health. Writing *Second Chances* was, she said, "a sort of exorcism" of her own fears of illness, specifically of cancer. Ten years before the publication of the novel Adams had experienced colon cancer, and in the interview she acknowledged the exorcism was successful on a private level.

An important question for readers of the novel to ask is whether Adams's imagined plight of the "almost old" works in the construction of a credible narrative in which the stories of San Sebastian residents offer fresh insights into universal questions about the human condition, particularly regarding aging. A majority of reviewers concluded that Adams succeeds in bringing these characters to life in *Second Chances* and that their stories transcend the rarified air of the affluent enclave of San Sebastian, offering universal observations about aging and about the value of friendship.

Tom Dowling, in a representative review, praised the novel in this way: "Time is the thief that takes us all by surprise, but somehow it seems to have sneaked up on Alice Adams with a vengeance."[13] Dowling here implicitly acknowledged that Adams, at a younger age than that of the characters she created, managed credibly to enter the psyches of these "almost old" characters in *Second Chances,* who, as Prufrock might say, have heard the eternal footman hold their coats and snicker. Dowling admired the fact that Adams "brought [all of the characters] to life with extraordinary precision and understanding,"[14] a point with which most of the positive reviewers agreed. Negative reviewers typically doubted that universal truths about aging could be inferred from the worries of those whose affluent lives set them apart from the rank and file of humanity. Adams believed that one could extrapolate truths from the dilemmas of those in San Sebastian, and in *Second Chances* she explores on several levels the intricacies of the friendships that bind the characters in the novel, relating their individual stories through flashbacks dating to the mid-1940s. She does this, however, only on the narrative's most superficial level. On a deeper level the novel brings the reader back time and again to this inescapable truth: when one is surrounded by longtime friends, they can add richness and excitement to life, but each individual must ultimately deal with the actuality of one's mortality—and with the loss of those to whom one has been close—alone. Adams argues through *Second Chances* that this fact has universal significance.

The novel opens with a New Year's Day walk in 1985 taken by the two closest friends in the novel, Dudley and Edward, who are both from Boston and who "have been friends 'forever'" (4); it is with their relationship that Adams frames her most probing interrogation of the subject of friendship. The novel ends with a New Year's Day walk one year later. On the first walk Dudley and Edward are discussing Celeste, who has recently lost Charles, her husband of nineteen years. She will join Dudley and Edward on their year-later walk in the last scene of the novel. From that first walk taken by Dudley and Edward, Adams manages through careful control of point of view to bring the "friendship" component of the novel into the foreground while maintaining the haunting "loneliness" undertone, and in that scene she establishes a pattern she will maintain throughout the rest of the novel.

Like most of Adams's novels, *Second Chances* is told from an omniscient point of view with close third-person narrative focus that shifts from one character to another as the novel progresses. In the first scene with Dudley and Edward the reader has access primarily to Dudley's thoughts, and as the two interact there is often a discrepancy between what they say to each other and what Dudley is thinking—about Edward, about what they have just said, and about subjects completely unrelated to their exchanges. Dudley is aware of the fact that she and Edward think alike on most things and even look a bit alike, but also she thinks about the fact that Edward's nose is ruddy and his hands shake because he drinks too much. She thinks, "Thank God [I don't] look like that" (4), although she would, of course, never express this to Edward. One would imagine that Dudley and Edward, as close friends for forty years, would find few subjects off limits. However, there are many subjects, such as Edward's homosexuality, that cannot be discussed; perhaps ironically, the two are able to talk about sexuality in general, but they are unable to speak of it in specific terms. In the course of their conversation, Dudley can (and does) think about sex in graphic terms, wondering what specific acts Celeste and her recent, mysterious younger boyfriend engage in, but she could never speak these thoughts to Edward. In their exchanges, Adams emphasizes the point that even the closest of friends have interior lives—fears and secret thoughts—that cannot be shared.

Dudley realizes, for example, that she can know only the specifics of her own sex life, though the reader learns later that even she and her husband, Sam, are not able to talk about sex openly because of their politeness. In fact, when Dudley returns home from her walk with Edward, the reader learns, again through access to her thoughts, that the dynamic of their verbal interaction is similar to that of Dudley and Edward. When she and Sam talk about Celeste and her boyfriend, Bill, Dudley realizes, "We are getting along better than usual," but she recalls with fear Sam's drunken rages of the past. They are never able to speak openly to each other about such things and are never "drawn to explicit conversations about the nature of their 'relationship'" (17).

Such recollections, however, do not prevent her from experiencing deep despair when he dies during the present year of the novel, despair compounded by the irritation she feels upon reading his will. Sam, as it turns out, was not particularly considerate of Dudley when he drafted it. Intimate thoughts such as those Dudley has had in the presence of her dearest friend, Edward, and also of her husband, Sam, are reflections Dudley would never share with them or with anyone else. The effect on her of this need to censor her innermost thoughts—and the effect of a similar reticence on virtually all of the San Sebastian friends and their close companions, who share Dudley's politeness in this regard—is that they all enjoy and gain benefits from their relationships, but they are all (Polly excepted) finally alone with many of their thoughts, anxieties, fears, and wishes. The result is loneliness, even in the presence of their friends and companions. A transcendent truth of the novel is that whatever a person's relationship to another—whether a best friend, a spouse, a partner, or a lover—some parts of the self remain incommunicable.

When the story moves forward into interactions between Edward and Freddy, his partner of thirty years, the dynamic of their communication is much the same as that between Dudley and Edward and between Dudley and Sam. The reader has access to Edward's thoughts in these exchanges rather than Freddy's, and Edward thinks to himself about how much closer to forty Freddy looks than to fifty, his actual age. But as the reader learns through Edward's thoughts, "For a variety of reasons [he] says none of this to Freddy" (27). When Edward learns that Freddy will leave to return to Mexico and teach American studies in the university, Edward would like to shout this to him: "Well, then go! If you are leaving, don't hang around. Just seeing you every day is a torment to me now. You constantly remind me of your absence." Of course, he cannot express his fear of abandonment so directly. He is left to deal alone with his despair, making him silent and "prey to the most dreadful imaginings, and impulses" (206). His kind of politeness is also evident in Celeste's exchanges with all of her San Sebastian friends, with whom she speaks in person and on the telephone, talking endlessly about superficial details of her life, including her relationship with Bill. But when she is back in her house or, in one case, has hung up the phone after talking with a friend, she is overtaken by uncontrollable despair that leads her to stand in her room and scream: "CHARLES! She screams and screams" (48).

Only mysterious Polly among these friends seems able to be direct in her communication with others, including these San Sebastian friends. Though not the novel's central character, Polly comes closest of all the characters to possessing in her later years the free, independent spirit as well as the openness that has characterized Alice Adams women in their prime—Megan Greene, for example. Back in the late 1940s, Polly, fresh out of Vassar, had an affair in New York with Charles, long before he met Celeste. She moved to Paris to be closer to him and became a smuggler for the Loyalist underground in Spain. Though the two continued to have a satisfying relationship, mainly dependent on their sex life, Polly realized she did not actually love Charles and was open and frank in telling him. Eventually, perhaps through coincidence, Polly, after a bout with cancer, winds up living close to Charles and Celeste in San Sebastian. Although there is a hint of suspicion on Celeste's part that Polly and Charles may once have been lovers, Celeste, in the name of politeness and for propriety's sake, never brings up the subject. As Charles suffers through his final illness, it is Polly who takes care of his physical needs when Celeste is unable to face the reality of his imminent death.

Then, during the year of the novel's present setting, when Celeste refuses to consult a doctor though she is obsessed with thoughts that she herself might have a terminal illness, only Polly will speak to her directly about it and convince her to have a full medical exam. And finally, when Polly begins an affair with the married handyman Victor, they talk freely and openly about all that is on their minds: "Victor talks to Polly like a man famished for conversation, ideas. . . . And she in turn talks to him; he is the only person in San Sebastian to whom she has recounted the true story of her time in Spain, those years of panic, occasional minor triumph" (201). Victor is Spanish, and when the two of them plan to go together to the European San Sebastian for a holiday, she freely tells her San Sebastian, California, friends about the plans—even arranges for Celeste to feed her cats while she is gone. It is through Polly that Adams comes closest in the novel to suggesting that there will be something of a happy ending for her free-spirited heroines in their older age. Polly becomes a vehicle in the novel through which Adams's own romantic sensibilities come through the novel's more prosaic and socially realistic surfaces.

In the novel's penultimate scene, Dudley, Edward, and, now, Celeste take the New Year's Day walk that parallels the opening scene of the novel, in which Dudley and Edward are walking across a field on the outskirts of San Sebastian, talking about their friend Celeste, who has just recently lost her husband and who, in Edward's words that day, "keeps reinventing her life" (3). During this last walk of the novel, the three of them are quite conscious of the recent news that Celeste's godchild/adopted daughter, Sara, whose story has been woven into a subplot of the novel, has been killed in a helicopter crash along with her lover while they were en route to a secret mission in Nicaragua. Celeste—true to her sense of politeness and propriety—wishes not to discuss this most recent, devastating loss. Instead, she points toward the "golden west": "But look, what a beautiful day this is," she says (255). And then after the walk, the three friends gather at Celeste's home for tea. Edward is smiling to himself over having just received a postcard from Freddy sent from Mexico, and Celeste and Dudley are delighted to share with Edward a card that has come from Polly in Barcelona announcing her and Victor's upcoming return. The three friends debate at the very end of the novel what sort of dinner they will have to commemorate Polly and Victor's return because, as they say, "It's always what we do, isn't it. Someone coming back from a trip?" They agree that they will limit the guest list to the five of them—Dudley, Edward, Celeste, Polly, and, since Sam has died during the year, Victor in his place—because that is who they have now: "just ourselves. . . . A little celebration" (257).

The novel ends on a note of what is, on one level, a powerful affirmation of the value of friendship: when a friend leaves for a time, there is comfort in the reconciliation ritual that commemorates the person's return and, in Polly's case, since she is returning with Victor, the welcoming of a new member into the circle of friendship. But as is true of virtually all of Adams's novels, the ending of *Second Chances* is filled with ambiguity and complexity. Unspoken in this last scene involving Dudley, Edward, and Celeste are truths that are doubtless present in the characters' thoughts, though absent from the words, of these three friends. For Dudley there will never be a reunion with Sam; for Edward, the closest he will come to a reunion with Freddy will likely be in the form of a postcard offering a glimmer of hope for Freddy's fragile health, in that he can send notes letting Edward know he is still able to make short trips, even though his AIDS has made improbable a return to San Sebastian; and for Celeste there will be no return of Charles.

As is true of virtually all of Adams's titles, this one, *Second Chances,* is resonant. It leads the reader to the heart of Adams's probing of eternal questions related especially to the role of chance in human destiny, particularly as the range of choices becomes increasingly narrow over the years, as death comes nearer and nearer. The reader is left to wonder whether one comes to deny the reality of losses that come with older age and to focus on the beauty of the present moment, as does Celeste, or whether one takes refuge in illusions based on slim hopes that come on postcards, as does Edward. Or there is also the option of taking refuge, as Dudley does, in one's work—which has been the salvation of earlier, younger Adams heroines. And finally, there is the option Polly chooses, that of taking a chance on romantic love and admitting openly to have done so, age be damned. Adams is by no means finished exploring possible alternatives for her characters, and many of them are yet to find their way into her short stories, as well as into her next novel, *Caroline's Daughters.*

CHAPTER 5

1980s Stories

To See You Again, Return Trips, and *After You've Gone*

While Adams enjoyed a successful career as a novelist during the 1980s, her life as a short story writer flourished. As she told Phil Thomas in an interview for the *Seattle Post-Intelligencer* in 1982 after publication of *To See You Again,* her second collection of short stories, "I put in about four hours a day writing. I have a short attention span so I often am working on a short story and a novel and, maybe a book review at the same time. I write about eight to 10 stories a year. A novel takes about two years."[1] And as it worked out from the publication of *Rich Rewards* (1980), her first novel of the decade, through *After You've Gone* (1989), her last story collection (and last book) of the 1980s, she published an equal number of novels and story collections (three of each) during that decade, although she often stated in interviews her preference for writing short stories over novels. Many of her stories through the 1980s appeared in the *New Yorker,* which had first refusal rights for each story she wrote; she had established a reputation as one of the nation's finest short story writers after the positive reception of *Beautiful Girl* (1979), a reputation that was secure by the time *To See You Again* appeared in 1982.

She had also begun teaching fiction writing at Stanford and at the University of California, Davis, and her experiences teaching—along with her critically acclaimed success—perhaps account for her increased willingness to discuss in interviews short story writing, about which she had clearly developed ideas that she enjoyed communicating to her students. An early mentor had taught her to use "an outline for writing short stories," and the outline came to serve as a rough guide for her in her own writing. It follows this pattern: A, B, D, C, E (action, background, development, climax, ending), an outline that Adams passed along to students and reported that she used regularly, especially when she was writing stories that covered years rather than days.[2] She had also been told early on in her career by a friend that she should never "pad" the soft edges of her fictional women—that she should "cut away at the soft edges . . . trying to get at the core of their lives."[3] Her stories are filled with characters whose soft edges have been cut away and who do not censor their feelings, and this is reflected in an important point that she tried to communicate to her writing students. In guiding one particular student in his development of a character in his story that was "misty and unclear," Adams told him this: "There should be absolutely nothing between her and what she's saying."[4] Adams was encouraging this student to "unpad" his character, to give her a kind of directness that Adams is so often praised for in the characterizations of her own fictional women. She wished to pass along to her writing students her belief that they should not feel obliged to follow "academic theories about the nature of fiction." Adams maintained that she did not have such "academic theories," a stance that led her to counsel her students to "think about what they read [and write] in terms of their own experiences, not in terms of abstractions."[5]

To See You Again (1982)

To See You Again appeared in 1982 and contains nineteen stories, nine of which had been published in the *New Yorker,* with the remaining ten having appeared in such places as the *Atlantic Monthly, Cosmopolitan,* the *Virginia Quarterly,* and *Shenandoah.* As had been true in the case of *Beautiful Girl, To See You Again* received more than two dozen reviews, a majority of which were positive and filled with praise for the elegance of Adams's prose and the stories' "perfect blending of form and content," in the words of one reviewer.[6] Most agreed that the stories in *To See You Again* are driven by Adams's focus on developing character and privileging that focus over plot.

As was true in the case of the stories in *Beautiful Girl,* the title story in *To See You Again* provides a helpful entry point into Adams's approach to character motivation and development in many of the other stories in the collection, and it does so in a way that leads back to Adams's ideas about getting "at the core" of her characters' lives. Laura, the story's main character and its first-person narrator, is teaching a class in freshman composition at Cornfield Junior College, east of her home in San Francisco. Hers is a one-semester job, and she drives to Cornfield and back home two days a week during the semester. The experience would be unexciting and uneventful—and likely not memorable or noteworthy—except for a student whose compositions suggest brilliance to Laura and whose youth and looks she is drawn to almost obsessively. Laura does nothing to act out her infatuation with Seth, the student, and realizes that from the moment he leaves class on the last day she will never see him again. The infatuation with Seth and Laura's thinking about it from every conceivable angle in the context of her present life give the reader a glimpse into Laura's character. In her own creative writing class Adams had counseled her student regarding the padding of his fictional character. And here in her own story Adams demonstrates precisely what this means: there is absolutely nothing between Laura in this story and what she is saying to the reader through her thoughts.

Laura recognizes that she is considerably older than the students in her class and "especially, cruelly, older than Seth" (291). Nevertheless, she is open to entertaining the fantasy of a romantic connection to him. This fantasy and Laura's contemplation of the many ways in which a relationship with Seth might evolve provide the reader a window on her present life, including her relationship both past and present with Gerald, her husband. In the present she thinks she must seem as old to Seth as she sometimes seems to herself—or as she sometimes imagines she must seem to Gerald. This leads her to thoughts of an older man who is attracted to her, an attraction that is analogous to her attraction to Seth. With these thoughts and with Seth's "face in my heart" (296), Laura approaches her home after her final day of class, soon to discover Gerald in one of his recurring states of serious depression, a condition that requires Laura to take him yet again for a stay at the small sanitarium that he goes to during such times. Driving home, Laura recalls when, as a student in Cambridge, she thought of Gerald romantically, much as she is now thinking of Seth. Gerald had been "so beautiful, so dark and thin, so elusive that I used to trail him around the Yard: me, a silly undergraduate with a crush on a future architect" (301). Finally at home, Claire pours a glass of wine and watches a play on television with an actor who reminds her of Seth, though he is much older—old enough to be Seth's father. In her mind she speaks to Seth: "Ah, Seth, at last you begin to lose your looks. . . . Now you are merely handsome, whereas before you were so beautiful that I could hardly look at you" (305).

Through Laura's fantasies about Seth and her associations to them, Laura reveals a complex self, a whole person capable of nurturing romantic idealism while also being capable of dealing in a practical way with the realities of her domestic situation, as well as with her own apprehension about aging. In the spirit of Adams's evolving sense of what constitutes strength in a contemporary woman, Laura lives consciously; she maintains her dignity, her romantic idealism, and her independent spirit, while tending to the practical demands of everyday life—and this includes work. Perhaps as important as any other quality, Laura sees herself across time: She is able to put her present fantasy regarding Seth in the context of her past (her past fantasies about Gerald, for example) and her future. She can project Seth into the future, and she can maintain hope for her relationship with Gerald and its difficulties, imagining that in Seth's prime and in Gerald and Laura's old age "Gerald will be completely well, the cycle [of his depressions] flat, no more sequences of pain. And maybe thin again. And interesting, and content" (305). In the end, as one might expect of an Alice Adams story, the conclusion is as complex and uncertain as contemporary life itself, a truth Laura contemplates in the story's final line: "It's almost worth waiting for" (305).

To See You Again is filled with stories containing main female characters like Laura, whose soft edges have not been padded. Fourteen of the stories in addition to the title story contain female characters who share Laura's directness and her openness to experience. Their backgrounds and their past experiences are different from Laura's, but all of the women characters are recognizable as the kind of strong, independent women who have come to be associated with the Alice Adams heroine. Their stories are, of course, all uniquely their own, as in the case of the narrator of "Greyhound People." As she regularly commutes on the Greyhound bus from San Francisco to her job in Sacramento, often taking by mistake the local bus rather than the express and often feeling an outsider among the more regular bus travelers, she feels isolated and marginalized. She is a recent divorcée who is dependent on rides to the bus station from her complaining housemate and on the goodwill of strangers, in this case a population of bus travelers who seemed to her at the beginning to be hostile and threatening. However, she is always sensitively taking in her surroundings, and the reader is privy to her constant, typically generous assessments of the people she encounters. By the end of the story she has gained freedom to interact joyfully with her environment, thanks in part to her decision to buy a bus pass to go "*anywhere in California*" (29); finally she is "considering the possibilities of California, which just then seemed limitless, enormous" (30). As Adams said of this woman "in transit from one part of her life to another," "Her reactions are stripped down. She is not in any shape to censor her feelings": she is, in Adams's words, "an unpadded person, which is to say unprotected."[7]

This narrator in "Greyhound People" is in at least some respects distinctly different from many of the female characters in *To See You Again,* most of whom are also "in transit from one part of [their lives] to another." Beyond the mention that the narrator is divorced, there is little reference to an earlier time in her life, an element that is present in many of the other stories—an element involving a backward glance that is often a "precipitating event" in the movement toward increased enlightenment for many of the characters. In the volume's title story, for example, the word "again" points to a past time when

Laura last saw Seth, even as it connects subtly to a time in the distant past when she first saw Gerald as she now thinks of Seth in the near past—connections Laura makes, signaling her ability to live consciously in the present.

Many of the stories in the collection mark changes in the characters and their discoveries by having them revisit actual places from their pasts—or by having them at least revisit these places mentally. This is evident in the three Hilton-related stories scattered through the volume—"An Unscheduled Stop," "A Southern Spelling Bee," and "Truth or Consequences"—stories that present a microcosmic view of the kinds of changes seen in the characters in the other stories in the volume. In the first of these, "An Unscheduled Stop," Claire Williston, a travel writer with a good magazine, is on a flight to Atlanta, which merely touches down briefly at the Raleigh-Durham airport, near Claire's childhood home in Hilton. The unexpected stop prompts memories of her growing up there and of "the searing love affair which took place on [her] last summer visit there" (65). In the end, she is able to gain strength by emotionally revisiting those memories from her past, and because she makes them conscious she manages to overcome the writer's block that her unscheduled stop had caused and is able to come back into the present with clear, sharp memories of places she had actually visited after the plane leaves the vicinity of Hilton and she goes on to San Francisco by way of Washington, D.C.

The second of the Hilton-related stories, "A Southern Spelling Bee," is told from an omniscient point of view and continues the narrative involving Avery of the Todd family sequence in *Beautiful Girl*. Now an adult living in San Francisco, Avery, who has been married several times and at present is married to a psychiatrist, has developed over the years into a thoughtful, mature adult. She appears now to comprehend the psychological dynamics of the twists and turns her life has taken in the years since her handsome distant relative, Cameron Lyons, set up a spelling bee between his daughter and Avery, who was more intellectually precocious than Cam's daughter. He made certain that Avery was given the most difficult words, while his "plump and pretty and blond" (195) daughter got only the simplest words to spell for his approval. Avery was finally driven to such frustration by this rigging of the spelling bee that she ran crying upstairs. Her real frustration was that she was unable to get from Cam the unconditional love that he so obviously gave to his daughter and that Avery very much wanted.

In the present, the grown-up Avery has invited Cam and his wife to dinner, noting on the telephone that her husband looks very much like Cam, an acknowledgment of the persistence in her memory of her desperate need for approval and love at that earlier time in her life. As she later asks her psychiatrist husband, finally sober after having drunk too much at dinner and having passed out at the table as Cam and his wife made numerous insensitive remarks, "Don't they know? How I must have felt about a little girl [their daughter] who could just smile to get love and not have to spell Constantinople?" (201). Avery's conscious acknowledgment and understanding of the lingering significance of that childhood moment of the spelling bee is evidence of her ability to revisit the past and incorporate it into her present many years later. She has changed from the Avery of "Alternatives" (*Beautiful Girl*), and she provides an excellent example of what Lee Upton referred to as Adams's use of "revisionary nostalgia," which Upton sees as "an active source of renewal"[8] for many of Adams's characters. In Avery's case the revisionary nostalgia is at once a source of renewal and a sign of Avery's maturity, evident in her open acknowledgment to herself and her husband of her conscious understanding of the relationship between her past vulnerability and her vulnerability in the present.

Although Adams's female characters make many different uses of nostalgia—not always involving renewal—there seems to be a common motivation that leads the characters to revisit the past. This motivation is directly expressed by Emily Ames in "Truth or Consequences," the third Hilton story in *To See You Again*. Emily is a northerner who has at the age of eleven moved to Hilton with her mother, and she finds herself years later reflecting on one especially memorable formative experience she had in her early days at school there. This experience involves a schoolyard game in which Emily, at that time an outsider because of her recent move to Hilton, has been trapped into admitting she would rather kiss Carstairs Jones, a social outsider and misfit who comes to school from the farm with his fellow "truck children," than be eaten alive by ants. In the end, Car, for reasons known only to him, violently, though privately, forces a kiss on Emily—her first kiss, which presumably only she and Car ever know about, and, after a brief period as a social outsider following this experience, Emily becomes assimilated into the highest ranks of Hilton's social order, finally leaving Hilton and eventually marrying a surgeon. Car Jones, fourteen years old and in the seventh grade at the time of the kiss, manages to test himself out of the seventh-grade class that he is too old for and advances to high school. He then enters the local university, where he turns down an invitation to join a prestigious fraternity, and goes on to distinguish himself as a playwright.

Emily has followed Car's life sporadically through relatives and from clippings forwarded by her mother. More recently, though, Emily has been startled to read in a gossip column that Car has married "a famous former movie star" (240). This bit of news propels Emily into the cluster of memories related to her early time in Hilton, particularly to her experience with Car Jones. She recalls the details of what actually happened in the "truth or consequences" episode, but more important is the way that she incorporates her understanding of the past into an understanding of herself in the present. Through her imaginative processing of her thoughts about Car, she comes to a deeper understanding of the experience than she had before. She begins to think of Car as having been in a situation similar to the one she was in when she first moved to Hilton, and she imagines all of the transitions that caused him to move from one step in his life to the next: he, like Emily, was a marginalized outsider, and because he found this status painful and unacceptable he took steps in his life to become a well-known playwright and, now, the husband of a famous former movie star. It is through Emily's empathizing with Car that she comes, in the last paragraph of the story, to gain insight into herself. She realizes that she could be completely wrong about Car and the things that motivated him. She could have completely misunderstood him. "He could be another sort of person altogether," she decides. And then she comes to the realization about her own motivation for revisiting the past in such elaborate detail: "he could be as haunted as I am by everything that ever happened in his life" (255). This realization opens Emily to an entirely different way of seeing her life both in the past and in the present.

The Hilton stories in *To See You Again* offer a useful introduction to the volume's remaining stories with female main characters who all share qualities with Claire, Avery, and/or Emily: Dylan Ballentine ("By the Sea"), Yvonne Soulas ("The Girl across the Room"), Janet Stone Halloran ("Lost Luggage"), Charlotte O'Mara ("Berkeley House"), Felicia Lord ("A Wonderful Woman"), Jane Phelps ("Legends"), Diana McBride ("Related Histories"), Cynthia ("The Break-In"), Maude ("True Colors"), and Amanda ("At the Beach"). Like Claire, many of these characters—Charlotte and Jane among them—are motivated to take control of their lives in the present by coming to a better understanding of shaping events in their past. Some, like Dylan, Janet, and Felicia, are, like Avery, moving toward greater understandings of themselves through examinations of their pasts. And most of them—Yvonne, Jane, and Diana included—are, like Emily, haunted by some past experience in their lives and gain empathy by understanding the experience. All are motivated to make discoveries, large and small, about themselves in the present so as to advance in the direction of increased self-knowledge and autonomy.

The four remaining stories in *To See You Again,* "Snow," "At First Sight," "The Party-Givers," and "Teresa," in different ways represent departures from the pattern in which a central character makes, in one reviewer's words, "discoveries and [takes] small steps toward enlightenment."[9] "Snow," the story Adams chose to lead off the volume, was first published in the *New Yorker* in 1979, and Adams perhaps selected it to open the collection because it establishes the groundwork for many of the eighteen stories that follow. The story appears at first glance to focus on the attempts of Graham to bring his daughter, Susannah, and Rose, her friend and lesbian lover, into closer touch with his life and with his own lover, Carol, a resourceful and independent San Francisco florist. As it turns out, the skiing on this trip is itself uneventful, and it appears at first to center on Graham's reflections on Susannah's childhood and the ways in which he could have been a better father. As the story evolves and after they return to their vacation house in Alpine Meadows after a day of skiing, the narrative moves in an entirely different direction.

"Snow" is, in fact, one of the stories reviewer Linda Pastan cites as one in which "nothing really happens . . . yet everything is revealed."[10] Graham overhears from the kitchen as he prepares dinner what begins as an amiable conversation among the three women. When he enters the room and moves close to Carol, he becomes a bystander in a discussion in which the three women recount defining experiences from their pasts. Rose reveals that she was raped as a young girl, and the assault has shaped the woman she has become, which, the reader understands, is at least in part a woman who needs a maternal presence like Susannah's in her life. Carol, in response to Rose's confession, admits to having become pregnant when she was fifteen and follows this with an insight: "You really can't tell what's happened to anyone" (13). Both Carol and Rose admit to regrets at not being able to go to college and having instead had to work, while Susannah reveals that she knows she has been privileged to have gone to Berkeley, her first-choice school—and, moreover, to be working in Los Angeles in films, as she always wanted to do. Graham comes to understand and accept that Susannah is closer to Rose than she is to anyone else; Susannah can be maternal, and Graham can now begin to fathom deep reasons that this is true. He also comes to perceive Carol as probably more beautiful than she was fifteen years ago, and this is likely because he has now seen her as a complex woman. All of them seem more authentic as individuals after they have interacted honestly with one another, and, ironically, Graham, one of only three main male characters in *To See You Again,* has perhaps learned more than anyone else about what can happen when individuals gain the strength to cut away their own soft edges. The story prepares the reader for the unpadding that will occur for many of the female characters that appear later in the volume.

Exploring further possibilities of what can happen when people drop their personas, a process that works to everyone's advantage in "Snow," Adams shows in "The Party-Givers" that the result is not always positive. Josiah in the story is a former alcoholic who enjoys giving parties at which all guests but himself drink too much and expose their uninhibited selves: "one of [his] eccentric theories about parties is that people should be uncomfortable, like prisoners; they are more apt to reveal themselves" (34). Josiah confirms his theory at his parties by providing only large quantities of cheap jug wine with very little food for his guests; he also consciously furnishes his flat on Potrero Hill in a minimalist fashion so that everyone will have to sit on the floor. As his parties are in progress, "[he] loves to watch [the guests]; he meticulously notes each stage of inebriation from the first slurred syllable to the final lurch toward the bathrooms" (42).

When the parties are over, he delights in discussing the bad behavior he has witnessed with his new wife, Hope Dawes, and his former lover, Clover Baskerville. Both Hope and Clover seem at first to share his dark passion for manipulating others for his amusement, though Hope's attachment to Josiah "is more like an insatiable greed, an addiction or perhaps a religious fervor" (32), a symptom perhaps of the malady that causes her constantly to contemplate suicide. However, she finds in the end that she may have gained the strength, the insight, and the distaste for Josiah's ways that allow her to imagine "a nice long trip to Bali, Tahiti, maybe, by myself" (45). Clover, a beautiful, promiscuous, and kind-hearted commercial artist, finds in the end that she is much happier with her generous employer, Gregory Rovensky, "a dark Russian-Israeli, an ebullient type" (36). He is a man who, though fat, bald, and physically unattractive, makes Clover much happier than Josiah and Hope ever did with their games. Both Clover and, finally, Hope have ironically gained strength at the end of the story by coming into close contact with and rejecting Josiah, whose Machiavellian manipulation of others satisfies his need to feel superior.

At the level of subtext, Adams condemns in "The Party-Givers" the exploitation of those who have, for whatever reason, been rendered defenseless; Josiah, because of his exploitative and manipulative nature, is one of the rare characters in Adams's fiction who is treated with no sympathy. The other two characters in *To See You Again* who warrant similarly unsympathetic treatment are John Conway and Posey McElroy in the volume's penultimate story, "At First Sight." The two, who are married to other people in the story's beginning—John to Althea, Posey to James—seem innocent enough at first. Posey, in fact, comes across to John's son Walker at first as beguiling—"the prettiest grown-up woman he had ever seen." She lavishes on Walker much-needed attention, in sharp contrast to his "somber mother" (280). John and Posey evolve, however, into villains who ultimately become responsible for the suicides of their mates, Althea and James. After years of seething over the treachery of his father and Posey, who married each other after the second suicide, and after the ending of Walker's love affair with Timothy, Walker returns to the beautiful but cold home his father had built, where Walker first met Posey. He discovers that the new owners have made the house warm, and they have a son, Paul, with whom Walker seems to fall in love "at first sight."

Adams sees nothing admirable in the behavior of John and Posey, and they join Josiah in the small gallery of Adams's irredeemable villains. The story, though, is more concerned with the relationship between romantic idealism and need. Walker was in such need of love early in his life that he initially idealized Posey, falling for her "at first sight" after she showered him with attention. His later love for Timothy appears based largely on the fact that Timothy, like Walker, had lost his mother to suicide—an apparent connection based on mutual need. In the final scene, in which Walker finds that the cold home of his youth has been made warm, Walker extends himself, arguably, out of a naïve need to revisit and revive a cold, dark part of his past: "for the second time in his life . . . his whole silly trusting heart rushes out, toward Paul, with love" (292)—Paul, the person who now occupies his old, cold bedroom, now warm. Here again, as she has done so often before, Adams interrogates the subject of romantic idealism, in this last scene especially, questioning the role of need in the process of falling in love. Adams leaves open the possibility that romantic idealism may be a foundation upon which one can build a relationship.

"Teresa," the antepenultimate story in *To See You Again,* is the volume's outlier, and Adams discussed it as such and in detail in interviews. In one interview Adams revealed that she wished "to break away from her past work in terms of locale and subject," and she cited "Teresa" as her most recent attempt to do this. She went on to explain that the story is based on a disturbing experience she had while visiting Mexico and hearing through friends the story of "a boy who was in jail for killing a man who had killed his father."[11] Adams visited the young boy several times in jail with her friends, once meeting his mother there. The mother was probably in her mid-thirties but appeared to be sixty. When Adams decided to write the story about the experience, she chose to present it from the mother's point of view, which meant that, as Adams said, she had to "put all I knew and much more into that story."[12]

The most dramatic events of "Teresa" involve the early courtship of Teresa by Ernesto, who defends her against the unwanted advances of Señor Krupp, owner of the plantation on which Ernesto works. Years after Teresa and Ernesto are married and after their children, including their son Felipe, are born and have become adolescents, Señor Krupp kills Ernesto when Ernesto again stands up to Krupp, who has killed Ernesto's friend. As the saga unfolds, Felipe exacts revenge for his father's murder by killing Krupp, an act that results in his imprisonment and ultimately in his death in jail—the spot at which Adams encountered the boy whose real-life story inspired "Teresa." The events of the fictional story have been filtered through the eyes and mind of the sensitive and observant Teresa, who from the beginning has had fears and misgivings related to the volatile Señor Krupp, the violent atmosphere that surrounded him, and the inequalities that are part of the plantation mentality. Teresa stoically endures all of this, but she is helpless to prevent the kind of violence that brings about the death of her husband, Felipe's need to exact revenge for the death of his father, and ultimately Felipe's death in jail. "Now I have no more to fear," she concludes. "Now everything has befallen me that possibly could, and for the rest of my days I am safe. I can go to sleep without fear." She decides to take her daughters to find a small beach hut to live in away from the oppressive atmosphere of the plantation: "We will live there together, by the sea, and grow old and be safe forever" (274).

In regard to locale and subject, "Teresa" differs from the stories that readers expect from Adams, and understandably she was disheartened when no magazine would accept it. As editors told her, "This doesn't sound like you."[13] In terms of theme, however, "Teresa" points to ideas Adams pursued from the beginning of her career: women who live in a patriarchal world with violence everywhere have legitimate reasons to be fearful, and they must often endure oppressive circumstances if they are to become independent, autonomous, and free of fear. The particular circumstances of Teresa's life amplify these circumstances, but they are present in more subtle forms in all of Adams's fiction. She would soon explore many of them on American soil in *Superior Women* and again on Mexican soil in several stories in her next collection, *Return Trips.*

Return Trips (1985)

After the publication of *To See You Again,* Adams published, to great fanfare (and large royalty checks), *Superior Women,* her 1984 best seller, and she also published stories regularly in the *New Yorker.* She was both professionally and financially secure. However, since 1982, as she confided in letters to Max Steele, her relationship with Bob McNie had not been going well; she was experiencing depression related at least partly to that relationship. Also, friends, acquaintances, and old lovers were confronting health problems, and some were dying. John Cheever, whose stories Adams had long admired, died in 1982, and by the end of 1984 Vasco Pereira, her married Portuguese lover, had died, as had Lavina Calvin, an older friend she had come to know through Mrs. Calvin's and her husband's associations with Bob McNie. Trummy Young, for whom she held deep affection and who had been the prototype for Jackson Clay in *Superior Women,* died shortly after Pereira. Adams dealt with the sadness of her losses during this time by immersing herself in writing—writing *Superior Women,* book reviews, and short stories, many of which came to be published in *Return Trips.* Six of the volume's fifteen stories appeared in 1983 and 1984 in the *New Yorker,* while four of the other fifteen appeared in other publications during these same two years. Contextualizing the stories in *Return*

Trips with these events in Adams's personal life helps readers understand the wistful mood of virtually all of the stories in the collection.

The title, *Return Trips,* points to a unifying subject for most of them. Virtually all of the stories contain characters who are traveling—taking trips—often from San Francisco to such far-flung places as Alaska, Portugal, Yugoslavia, Mexico, New Mexico, North Carolina, Massachusetts, the Santa Cruz Mountains, and Carmel, California. Most often the trips are actually taken by the main characters in the stories, though sometimes the main characters experience them only vicariously or in their imaginations. And quite often, though not always, the trips are literally "return trips": the characters are going back to places where they had once been—places that have lodged, for good or for ill, in their memories; in some cases they are trips to locations to which the main characters will not, for understandable reasons, physically return. As was true of all of Adams's book publications after *Careless Love, Return Trips* was reviewed widely, and, with rare exceptions, the collection was received favorably and enthusiastically by reviewers in publications as diverse as the *New York Times Book Review,* the *Washington Post, Gay Community News, San Francisco Chronicle, Belle Lettres,* the *London Times,* and more than a dozen other publications. Many of the reviewers alluded to the recurrence of the "trips" motif in most of the stories in the collection. This traveling motif is more important in *Return Trips* than in many of Adams's other works because of the clear resonance in each story of the word "trips." As one reviewer expressed it, "Naturally, the 'trips' described [in this volume] are emotional as well as physical."[14]

Perhaps even more important in the case of many of the stories in the collection is the idea not only that the trips have significance for the characters on a literal level but that as "*return* trips" they work also on a more complex metaphorical level. They become more than literal trips. The book's title, *Return Trips,* itself sets a mood that is at once wistful and nostalgic, while it at least also hints at the potential for hope in the return. Rarely, however, are the emotions of the main characters in these stories simple enough to be contained in either of the words "wistful" or "hopeful." More often the characters experience a range of emotions related to the journeys or trips—real or imagined—that they take. The title story, "Return Trips"—like the title stories of the other collections—provides a useful window for examining the range of complex emotions often experienced by the main characters in the other stories in the volume. One of the most intricate and carefully layered stories in the collection, "Return Trips" follows Emma, the first-person narrator, through trips to Europe (real and anticipated), trips back and forth between New York and Washington, D.C., and many trips—most of them imaginary, though the final one is real—back to Hilton, the town where she grew up. The two most important trips of Emma's life come at the beginning of the story and at the end. The first takes place in the distant past, "some years ago" (24), when Emma was in Yugoslavia with the love of her life, Paul, who died young; the second occurs in the present, near the end of the story: it came "last June, when I [Emma] had agreed to give a series of lectures at Georgetown," after Emma decided on an impulse to return to Hilton for a visit of several days (37).

During the course of time, between these literal trips, the reader also follows Emma on journeys through many years of her life, through several love affairs, through two marriages, and into a successful career as a scholar, author, and lecturer, married in the present to a successful doctor. But the two bookend trips are tied to the most important events in Emma's emotional life—or are at least directly connected to them—and thematically they are the most important trips of the story. Years before the present time of the story, Emma spent the hot summer in an ugly yellow hotel in Yugoslavia accompanied by Paul, with whom she had traveled from New York. This trip is important for several related reasons, the first of which relies on what Emma refers to as her "magic belief" that marrying Paul would "cure" him. She believed that she would be able to heal Paul's congenital heart condition through her great love of him and his love of her. However, knowing he would die young, Paul insisted that she leave him in Europe, go back to America, and pursue her graduate degree. The summer in Yugoslavia is memorable because of the miserable heat and Paul's condition, but it is significant mainly because it marks the end of the most important relationship in her life. Emma is haunted from that time until the present by the thought that she left Paul to die in Europe, which he did, soon after she left, in Trieste. The trip takes on further importance after, one night while in bed with Paul, she has a horrible dream about Hilton, a dream in which she cannot, because of a deep pain in her chest, make it down the hill to the big white house that was her childhood home. The dream operates on two levels that finally unite the many threads of the story. Most obviously, in the dream Emma wishes to make it to her house to help repair her parents' relationship. She is unable to do this in the dream and in reality, and she moves away from Hilton to Washington with her mother and father, who soon dissolve their marriage. The dream also involves her deep knowledge that the problem of Paul's heart, coded in the dream as her own heart, is an obstacle magical thinking cannot overcome.

By establishing in the first Yugoslavia scene with Paul the two components of Emma's life that remain unresolved until her actual trip to Hilton near the end of the story, Adams creates the foundation on which she constructs the narrative of Emma's complicated life. The strands of the story involve graduate school, marriages, and professional advancement, all connected by her lingering regret over her inability to cure Paul's heart condition and over her having left him in Europe to die. Sadness remains, of course, over the fact that she was never quite able to heal her parents' relationship in Hilton, in that "romantic and exciting" home of her youth (27). Her literal trip to Hilton near the end of the story becomes the trip that allows her to engage in the constructive process of combining actual memory with wishful thinking, while placing both in the context of present reality. Once back in Hilton, she discovers it to be, in fact, a real rather than a magical place. The house of her youth "had been repainted—all smartened up with bright white paint and long black louvered shutters." (40). And she finds Popsie Hooker—a person connected long ago to her parents and a person with whom she had often pleasurably corresponded—to be much less enticing than the enchanted being of her memory and of their correspondence. Popsie is in reality a racist and a snob. On her flight back to New York, Emma becomes "aware of an unusual sense of well-being . . . at peace, and ready for whatever should come next" (43). What is, in fact, to come next as she looks to the future is a trip with her husband to Europe, a trip that will take them close to Trieste, where Paul died. But she feels no need to visit Trieste or to make a return trip to Yugoslavia and the yellow hotel in which she and Paul had spent their last time together. Rather, she very much "like[s] the idea of just being in its vicinity" (44).

Emma is able to reach the state of peace she has attained at the end of "Return Trips" by finally returning to the actual place she always considered home and integrating the mythical home of her memory—now almost unrecognizable—into the reality of her present life and even into the more distant life of her past relationship with Paul. She has learned to accept the mutability of the past and the role of imagination in shaping her memories, keeping in mind the reality of her life in the present. The peaceful endpoint Emma comes to is very much like the one in which the narrator finds herself in the story/autobiographical sketch "My First and Only House" (the last story in *Return Trips*), which emphasizes the importance to Adams of the returning-home process—a process that many of the return trips in the collection share. In this sketch the narrator speaks of the house in which she grew up in Chapel Hill, a house she revisited—for the first time in decades—shortly before she wrote this piece, in this way: "I am visited there in dreams by the present-day population of my life"—and one could add by characters in her stories as well—"[by] people who in fact have never been to that hilltop where the house was—where it *is*" (190). Then she finishes the sketch with an acknowledgment that the house as it is in the present, like the house in "Return Trips," is freshly painted and bears little resemblance to the actual house she grew up in but that this present house "is not where I live. I live in a huge, mad house with the loveliest view. With everything in bloom" (195). In other words, her home and her town are the home and town of her memory, "in which I spent my first sixteen years" (191). Adams's main characters can be selective in how they use this home of memory. They can revisit it and draw strength from the good memories, while acknowledging the reality that it contains unpleasant memories, too. As the narrator says in "My First and Only House," "It is strange to me that I am so fixed, so literally rooted in a house of which my memories are not of a very positive nature on the whole" (194); however, thanks to the "vagaries of memory" the house has a lovely view "with everything in bloom" (195).

It has been apparent in many of Adams's previous works that the past is to her a living thing, and nowhere more than in the stories in *Return Trips* does it become clearer that her characters can relate to and use this living past in a variety of ways, some constructive and some less so. The two stories already examined, "Return Trips" and "My First and Only House," provide the volume's best examples of constructive processing of the past in that both narrators have transferred their wistful longings for home—memories that possessed them—into agents of personal growth. Both have used their nostalgia in a way Lee Upton has characterized as "revisionary," which is to say they have revised the living past in a way that leads to a better understanding and acceptance of their present lives. Appearing as they do near the beginning and near the end of *Return Trips,* these stories serve as a useful frame—and as frames of reference as well—for the other stories in the collection, seven of them in addition to the two discussed representing trips that contain at least some degree of reconciliation for the main female characters in the stories: "New Best Friends," "Time in Santa Fe," "A Public Pool," "Barcelona," "Mexican Dust," "Elizabeth," and "Sintra."

Of the six remaining stories ("Alaska," "You Are What You Own: A Notebook," "La Señora," "Waiting for Stella," "Separate Planes," and "Molly's Dog"), "Molly's Dog" best illustrates the way in which lack of reconciliation operates in the other stories. A key to this lack of reconciliation is found in an allusion to E. M. Forster's novel *Howards End,* which the title character Molly is rereading and which she plans later to take with her, as she waits for her gay friend Sandy to pick her up for their planned weekend in Carmel. As reviewers pointed out, the lines from the novel provide a point of reference for Molly's near-despair in the story. She is unable to follow the imperative of the novel's epigraph and the guiding light of the novel's main character: "Only connect." On many levels Molly is unable to connect—to Sandy in the present or to the dog she and Sandy leave in Carmel. The dog—"Molly's dog"—is symbolic of the old past life of passion that she knew years ago in Carmel with lovers long before the trip that she and Sandy take in the story.

From the beginning Molly realizes on some level that her planned trip with Sandy, whom she has known for many years, is a mistake. She awakes from a nightmare the evening before their planned trip, envisioning how awkward it will be to be in "tawdry" Carmel, she "a scrawny sun-dried older woman" with "her wheezing, chain-smoking, fat queer friend" (120). It will be awkward, and they will drink too much, she knows. She also then recalls an earlier romantic trip some years before when she and her lover entered their cabin, perhaps the same cabin she and Sandy will be occupying, and immediately had sex instead of drinking too much. The next day, as she waits for Sandy to arrive, she becomes irritated with his lateness, which leads her to begin rereading *Howard's Inn*. Finally, as she and Sandy make the journey to Carmel, Molly's spirits lighten a bit, though she cannot keep from thinking about how different the trip is from the earlier times when she went to Carmel with lovers. She rationalizes that the Molly of those days was a "very silly early self of hers" (125).

On the river beach the next day, they encounter the dog of the story's title, which attaches itself to Molly and Sandy, and Molly begins enjoying herself. She also begins focusing her attention on the dog, which follows them even as they leave in the car. She sees the dog racing behind them, and "Molly closed her eyes, aware of violent feelings within herself, somewhere: anguish? dread? She could no more name them than she could locate the emotion" (129). Sunday morning when the two leave Carmel, Molly becomes impatient with Sandy because he has been insensitive in not returning to see if the dog is on the beach. During the trip back to San Francisco they become openly hostile to each other, she calling him "selfish" and he calling her "stupid." They both apologize before they reach San Francisco, but their relationship has been damaged, never to be fully repaired. As time passes Molly thinks back on Carmel "in a vaguely painful way, as a place where she had lost, or left something of infinite value. A place to which she would not go back" (134). On the most obvious level she has lost her friendship with Sandy in Carmel; on another, she has left the dog there, but the reader understands that the dog is a creature onto which Molly has projected her greatest loss: the loss of her young, romantic self. Her knowledge that she will not go back indicates that she cannot incorporate her past—or, more precisely, her memory of herself in the past in Carmel—into the person she has become. She is finally unable to reconcile her two selves.

Molly's plight is similar to that of the other characters in the nonreconciliation stories—Lucille Lawson in "Alaska," for example, who remembers she lived in Alaska with the first of her five husbands—"the worst, by far," she thinks—but she "sometimes feels a confusion in her mind about which husband she will meet, at the end of the day." Lucille "feels the presences of those other husbands lurking in her mind but none of them was worth a whole lot, come to think of it" (3). Literal visits or vicarious ones would serve little purpose in helping Lucille reconcile her present self with the selves of her past. They remain distant to her and largely unknown. Similarly disconnected from one another and from parts of themselves, the almost very old guests in "Waiting for Stella" appear symbolically to be waiting for the dead Stella to actually appear at dinner. They are unable to imagine their lives without her. It seems unlikely that any of them will experience the peace of reconciliation because they remain statically fixed in a past when Stella was actually alive. The characters in these nonreconciliation stories are simply unable to connect—with other people or with parts of themselves from which they remain detached. As Adams herself reached a time in her life when she was, like Molly, "not twenty any more, or thirty or forty, even" (121), she became increasingly interested in the process by which people do or do not make connections—with other people, with their pasts, with their memories. The stories in *Return Trips* represent Adams's most concentrated effort to explore this process in fiction, though she would revisit the subject both in her next novel, *Second Chances,* and in many of the stories that appear in her fourth story collection, *After You're Gone.*

After You've Gone (1989)

Adams wrote the fourteen stories in her fourth short story collection, *After You've Gone,* in "a three- or four-year period during which [she] was also working on novels."[15] This was true partly, as she put it, because "I have a very short attention span. . . . I need the stories to divert me when I'm working on a novel."[16] This "three- or four-year" timeline suggests Adams wrote most or all of the stories in the collection during the time she composed her sixth novel, *Second Chances* (1988), which immediately preceded *After You've Gone,* and her seventh novel, *Caroline's Daughters* (1991), which she had already written and was revising when the short story collection appeared. This is useful information for the reader of *After You've Gone* because it helps explain the dominant mood of uncertainty felt by the characters in many of the stories, much as events in her life leading up to the publication of *Return Trips* helped explain the wistful mood of the stories in that collection. As Adams said, some of the stories in *After You've Gone* were "written during a period of discouragement." When pressed to explain whether this discouragement is related to "man-and-woman matters," Adams responded in this way: "I write about what I feel and see, and I don't see much that I find cheering. Between men and women today I see distrust, anger and loneliness on both sides. It's a discouraging scene. It must be worse for people who are much younger."[17] It is fair to say that Adams herself was in a period of transition when she wrote the stories in *After You've Gone,* her personal transitional state related both to her reflections on growing older herself and to her concern about the future of her relationships during and after the severing of her close ties with Bob McNie. Her reflections and thoughts on these subjects find their way into stories in the collection, much as her reflections on loss played a role in determining the direction of many of the stories in *Return Trips.* As she admitted in a candid moment following the publication of *After You've Gone,* "I think the truth about writing stories is that I take emotions of my own and attach them to made-up people."[18] As it turns out, each of the stories in *After You've Gone* explores Adams's thoughts and feelings—expressed through "made-up people"—about what it means to exist in a state of transition like the one Adams was in between the years of the composition of *Second Chances* and the publication of *After You've Gone*—a liminal space that virtually every character in the story collection finds her- or himself in at one time or another.

The title story, "After You've Gone"—the only title story in any of the collections that Adams places first in a volume—is an important one generally in Adams's short story canon because it treats so many of the subjects that she had dealt with to this point, both in her stories and in her novels. Most obviously the story deals with love, loss, regret, and recovery—both the narrator's past love for the poet-lover who has abandoned her for a younger woman named Sally Ann and for the developing love of a friend the narrator knew in her college days. In her frank letter to the poet-lover who has left her—the letter is the story itself—the narrator is quite open in acknowledging the things she misses in their relationship: she misses his cooking, his ability to fix broken things, and his poems. As the letter demonstrates, she is able, as are many of Adams's earlier characters, to nostalgically revisit the past, accept it, and integrate it into her present life: "I do miss it all, the house-fixing and cooking, the love and the poetry. But I did very well without it all" (6). The qualifying verb "did" in this case prepares the reader for the narrator's indictment of the poet-lover that is to come in the letter and for the narrator's request that he free his new love, Sally Ann, from her unhappy situation by turning her loose.

Like many of Adams's most admired characters, the narrator of "After You've Gone" has little patience with her former poet-lover when she perceives she is being entangled in an abusive relationship—as, in truth, she is, in an indirect way in the present and as she was perhaps entangled when she and her poet-lover were together. The poet-lover's new love is inundating the narrator with letters suggesting that she (the narrator) is being held up to Sally Ann as a model because she, unlike Sally Ann, is a professional (a lawyer) who values work and has a purpose in life. These letters are not tolerable to the narrator because she sees injustice in the poet-lover's treatment of Sally Ann, whom he manipulated to satisfy a passing fancy, much as the narrator now likely imagines the poet-lover manipulated her in the past. In the interest of moving forward with her own life, the narrator must remove herself from her role in this triangular relationship so that she can again go back to doing "very well without it all" and moving forward with her life and her present hope for a new love and satisfying work with her self-esteem intact—a situation that Adams's strongest, most sympathetically drawn women seek to inhabit. The use of the epistolary form in "After You've Gone" is an unusual departure for Adams, and her reference to Sally Ann's letters to the narrator is effective in providing a plausible motive for the narrator's response by letter to her former lover. Adams's leaving opens up the question of whether the narrator actually sends her letter to the poet-lover, a feature of the story that underlines the uncertainty associated with liminal states examined throughout the collection. Thematically Adams is here exploring strategies for dealing with feelings of abandonment while refusing to deny the happiness that preceded the abandonment. The narrator's triumph is in her discovery of the human potential to move the pain of loss into the present and future without denying the existence of the romantic idealism that first drew her to her poet-lover.

In its placement as the first piece in the volume, "After You've Gone" sets a tone of both uncertainty and irony for the stories that follow. "Your Doctor Loves You," the last story in the volume, is a complement to it, and together they nicely frame the collection. The situations of the two main characters are similar in that both characters have been left by men. In the case of Holly Jones in "Your Doctor Loves You," the man who has left her is her husband, Sebastian. Holly, though, is at an early stage of grief, which at the beginning of the story "was severe." In the terrible days and weeks, "then months," following her abandonment, she has long talks in her head with Sebastian—no letter writing or actual conversations, as in the case of the narrator of "After You've Gone." Holly's talks in her head after her abandonment are "a terrible mix of cold analysis and warm vituperation, often with more than a little scalding lust thrown in" (205). At last she decides to move forward with her life, gets a lawyer to arrange a divorce, and gains some peace. She seeks out an old friend, Mary, who convinces her that their physician, Dr. Jonathan Green, might be romantically interested in Holly, a bit of fantasy that leads to the situation that sets up the story's final ironic turn.

In the end, for all of Holly's preoccupation with making herself desirable for Jonathan Green, it turns out that he is drawn to much younger women and that his interaction with Holly is primarily professional, doctor-to-patient. On the occasion of their one dinner date at Holly's house, the two "neck" like teenagers on the sofa, but, after later bringing her medicine to treat her illness, he sends her a bill for a "House call and follow-up treatment. One hundred dollars" (229). By the time she receives this bill, however, Holly has regained her perspective in relation to her loss of both Sebastian Jones and Jonathan Green. She and Mary are able to laugh and joke about the experience with the doctor, and Holly has hung up the phone on Sebastian when he calls her drunk in the middle of the night, thus signaling an end to her participation in an abusive relationship. She realizes that she "wouldn't dare say that the pain is absolutely gone, very likely . . . it won't ever be" (227), but she is able to return to the past in her mind and integrate it into her present—always a step in the right direction for Adams's female characters who are regaining their self-esteem.

These two stories frame the twelve others in the collection, in which main characters are in uncomfortable, often intolerable, situations that seem to call for change either in the character's literal circumstance or in her attitude, though a change does not always take place. Virtually all of these characters are in a liminal state and faced with the dilemma of what they will do "after" leaving this liminal state—or, in some cases, what will be the consequences of remaining in this state for an extended period of time. The situations and subsequent in-between states are not necessarily prompted by dramatic events such as divorces or breakups, though many of the characters feel they have been emotionally deserted and are living in empty relationships in which they feel isolated. Perhaps the most powerful example of such a relationship—and one in which the choices appear limited—is "1940: Fall," in which Caroline Coffin Gerhard has grown accustomed to the absence of her husband, Arne, who is on a visiting faculty appointment in California, away from the family's home in Madison, Wisconsin. From all indications Caroline and Arne's relationship has not been good for some time. She has assumed he is unfaithful and has come to resent his returns, which come on short notice and seemingly only at times convenient to him. She has had the responsibility of raising their three children—two adolescents and one still an infant in 1940.

A responsible mother, Caroline has nevertheless become increasingly interested in living a life independent of her husband. She likes taking walks alone and having time to write letters to newspapers about the current world situation. She is weary of immersing herself in what she has come to see as the self-absorption of adolescents (that is, the lives of her children and their friends). In effect, she is trapped in the confines of motherhood, in a marriage without love, unable to pursue her interests in any way other than through writing letters to editors about her political concerns, in this time mainly involving her fears about the dangers of Hitler. As she writes her letters, her garden wilts, and she sleeps better "not having to worry about the other's sleep," and she tells herself she "should not have Arne so continually in my mind" (24). Unlike the narrator in "After You've Gone," Caroline remains in her state of uncertainty until Arne dies, in the 1950s. In the story's present time of the 1980s, when Caroline is in her eighties and has had both tragedies and triumphs with her children, she continues to write political letters to newspapers, members of Congress, and senators—even attends demonstrations—and she is, according to her son-in-law, "still very much alive" (28). From all evidence she has remained in the liminal state she was in during the fall of 1940, and the reader must determine whether her decision to stay in her relationship with Arne until he dies is a decision that was finally in her best interest. She is, after all, "still very much alive" in her eighties, but for the reader acquainted with Adams's sense of irony and her belief in the importance of gainful employment that provides independence, there remains the question of what Caroline may have given up in the pursuit of love or a profession or self-esteem as she remained in that liminal space of marriage to Arne until later, through death, he was "gone."

In a short final section of the narrative headed "Epilogue: San Diego, California. The middle eighties," the reader learns that Caroline's youngest daughter, "Baby," has died of a drug overdose in the early 1960s; the oldest has been married three times; and the middle child has earned a Ph.D. in math and is happily married to an exchange student she met in the fall of 1940. Caroline lives with the couple, as we learn through a character that seems an Adams persona, Lauren Whitfield. Lauren is a successful psychologist specializing in alcoholism and codependent relationships; she has been married twice; and she still dreams of the boy she went steady with in the fall of 1940, a young man with whom she broke up after he drunkenly mistreated her during her visit to Madison, where she came to know the Gerhards. By intertwining the stories of Caroline, her children, and Lauren throughout the story—and emphasizing it in the epilogue—Adams underlines the point that uncertainty in relationships extends across time, far beyond the fall of 1940, treating it as a complex problem with no easy answers.

This epilogue also foreshadows the anger and distrust of a younger generation that she explores in "Child's Play," the only Hilton story in *After You've Gone.* With the story title Adams calls attention to the two actual children, Prudence Jamieson and Laura Lee Matthews, whose playing together a "long time ago, in the thirties" allowed them to form "a balanced, exceptionally happy friendship" (46) that would endure into the present, even as their adult parents were playing destructive, childish games. While all four of the parents become alcoholics, only Sophia, Prudence's mother, drinks her sherry alone in her room, largely, it appears, because she has been driven to despair by living in a loveless relationship with Dan, her professor husband, who flirts shamelessly with Liza, Laura Lee's mother. Though there are other complicating factors the text only hints at, it appears Sophia deals with the despair of not knowing what to do—her in-between state—by secretly drinking herself to an early death, as it turns out only a few years after Liza has died of "liver problems" caused by her own drinking. Following a pattern similar to that of the children who survived into adulthood in "1940: Fall," the main characters in "Child's Play," Prudence and Laura Lee, have found different ways in their adult lives of surviving their parents, who acted like children "a long time ago, in the thirties" when Prudence and Laura Lee were growing up. Prudence has become a physicist and teacher, and Laura Lee has become an alcoholic, married three times and now living back in her family home in Hilton. They are members of the younger generation reaping the consequences of their parents' child's play, remaining "close friends, not seeing each other often but phoning . . . just to keep in touch—drunken Laura Lee and terribly sober Prudence, laughing like children" (60).

Two of the other stories in the collection depict women who are in unhappy relationships with their husbands, as Caroline is with Arne and as Sophia is with Dan. In "The End of the World" Zelda Hoskins is on vacation in Mexico with Abe, her husband, but much of her time and energy are spent composing and writing letters to her lover, a computer salesman from New York, who visits her in Toronto from time to time. She has told him often that their relationship must end, but they seem always to wind up in bed together when he comes to Toronto, leaving her in a seemingly endless in-between state with both her husband and her lover. In "On the Road," Brendan Hollowell, a successful and much sought-after "feminist" lecturer on a book tour to promote her recent *Sex and Creativity,* is married to a man who seems disconnected from her and her career. As she sees it, "he is often distracted, his mind somewhere else, presumably his work" (157), and "they do not—ever, quite—communicate" (140). She imagines that there might be other women in his life, and she is in a state of uncertainty as to whether he still loves her. For her part, while on the road she is always on the lookout for a man she might connect with—an old friend or a new one—though she typically winds up alone, lonely, and insecure. After one of her lectures, these words keep going through Brendan's mind as she lies sleepless in her luxurious suite: "Why am I doing all of this?" (149) As in so many of Adams's stories, the reader is left at the end in a state of uncertainty as to the future of Brendan's tenuous relationship with her husband. For the reader, there is finally the lingering question as to why either of them is "doing all of this" and whether Brendan will rise to the occasion at some point in the future and find the courage to leave her uncertain state, as do so many of Adams's strong women, and to regain the independence she had in her graduate school days when she was just beginning her studies of "creative women" (139).

Three of the other relationships in *After You've Gone* involve women who are not married to their lovers. In all three relationships the women are in transitional situations similar to those of Caroline and Zelda. In "What to Wear" Sheilah Cullan remains emotionally connected to her verbally abusive lover, with no end in sight. As the story opens, she is contemplating which outfit she should wear to please him when she visits him in a mental institution, Adams here making a point about the control one person can exert over another when one surrenders her or his independence. In "Fog," artist Antonia Love is in a transitional phase both with her young, unfaithful lover and with her career. She resolves the situation at least temporarily by making plans to leave San Francisco, which she says she hates, and heading off to Wyoming with the unpredictable lover. She convinces her friends, though not the reader, that "Antonia Love these days is a very happy woman" (77). And in "Travelling Together," the story perhaps closest to "After You've Gone" in suggesting that there can be hope for a life beyond entrapment in an unhappy relationship, Susan Quince is traveling in Europe with Ralph, her volatile lover. They quarrel before leaving on the trip as well as during the time they are away; in one instance, when they are given a room with twin beds, they "find themselves defeated, always, in terms of sex, by separate beds" (198). Susan bears the discomforts of their relationship because Ralph's simple presence helps her with her anxiety and her panic attacks, particularly on plane trips. On the flight back from Milan to the United States, there is turbulence, and Susan's terror is lessened by Ralph's presence. She thinks, "I can never leave him, I will never find the nerve" (204). In a single line that reminds the reader that the story has been told in flashback, the reader learns that "a few years later . . . Susan had managed, at last, to sever ties with Ralph for good" (201), an outcome that marks her as a strong Adams character.

The two stories in the collection with male protagonists ("Ocracoke Island" and "A Sixties Romance") also depict characters in liminal spaces and reflect Adams's observation that the unhappiness she sees in contemporary relationships is shared by men and women. These two stories, however, tend to reinforce the point made by many of the reviewers of *After You've Gone*—a majority of whom praised the volume—that the men in most of the stories are unsympathetic. In the case of "Ocracoke Island" Duncan Elliot, the main character, is a distinguished, aging professor emeritus at a midwestern university and has just been abandoned by his young third wife, who has run off to Ocracoke Island with a visiting poet. Adding to his discomfort over the abandonment, Elliot has suffered a broken tooth on a trip to New York, where he visits with an old student, an erudite literary critic, and his second wife, Emily. Elliot's plight is lamentable to the reader, but during each of the encounters the reader discovers that many of his wounds have been self-inflicted. He has, for example, had numerous, if "minor," "dalliances himself (127); he had actually suggested at one point that his wife have an affair; and he was responsible for sending her off to the reading that resulted in her running away to Ocracoke with the visiting poet. Moreover, he seems more worried about the impression he has made on his former student (now successful in the advertising world), the literary critic, and Emily than he is about the fact that his wife has left him. In short, he comes across as narcissistic and pompous. The reader, though, cannot finally avoid feeling some sympathy for this man who is not completely at the end of his career but who is no longer the admired mentor to his former student. The sympathy Adams elicits for him at the end of the story is for his "whole tormented landlocked soul" (137) that can never go to Ocracoke Island, which has become a metaphor for his lost youth.

Adams offers no such grounds for sympathy for architect Roger Michaels in "A Sixties Romance." Roger is "accustomed to being attractive to women" (159)—and his awareness of this fact when he first meets Julia Bailey makes his attitude toward her—a mathematician, a Stanford professor, and "a generous woman" (165)—all the more offensive to the reader. From the beginning he thinks "she's not up to my usual standards"—"not even as good-looking as my former wife" (159). Quite to his surprise, Roger falls in love with Julia—with her lovemaking, her cooking, her generosity, her trusting nature. And then as time passes he begins to take Julia for granted. He observes to himself how difficult "those sixties years were . . . on middle-aged men": "Young girls were everywhere with dresses up to there, and the longest, thinnest legs, lightly tanned. And breasts: so many girls going braless" (170). Roger succumbs to temptation and begins to have romantic meetings with young, married Candida, who makes him feel young.

After one of the trysts in a motel with Candida, Roger carelessly leaves the motel bill in his car; Julia finds it, and this sets up the poetically just ending of the story (which Adams actually reveals to the reader in the story's first paragraph): "Julia was the last to break his heart" (159). She will have nothing more to do with Roger after her discovery of the motel bill, and Adams presents two alternative ways that Roger could conceivably deal with his loss of a woman he continues to love, could deal with his loss "after she's gone": he could be "pained by songs that brought her back"—songs they had listened to together—or he could fall back into his old habit of foregrounding her faults in his mind. He chooses the latter, and, instead of remembering the love they shared and her beautiful smile, he sees only the scars he had at first noticed on her face: "deep, irremediable scars" (180). With this choice Roger is thrown back into the habit of mind that will protect him from ever having his heart broken again. Since Julia was "the last to break his heart" (157), the reader assumes that he closes himself off forever to the possibility of love. In this closing off, Roger commits what is in Adams's world something close to the unforgivable sin, and Roger becomes one of the few characters in Adams's fiction who is presented as an individual with few, if any, redeemable qualities.

The three outliers in *After You've Gone*—the stories in which the conflict is not centered primarily on individuals and their wives, husbands, or lovers—are clustered in the center of the volume: "Lost Cat," "Tide Pools," and "Favors." In all cases, however, the characters in these stories, like those in the other eleven, are experiencing moments of uncertainty in their lives and are faced with the dilemma of whether to accept their situations or to take steps to move beyond them. In "Lost Cat," Maggie is in despair over the possible loss of her missing cat, Diana, until the cat returns and Maggie realizes that she has projected all of her fears in life—of cancer, of the possible loss of her boyfriend, among others—onto Diana, an insight that allows her to move beyond the liminal space she was in before her "lost cat" experience. In "Tide Pools" Judith Mallory resolves her lonely existence in which she is teaching marine biology in Minnesota, far from the sea, by returning to Santa Barbara, the home of her youth. Ostensibly she moves back to Santa Barbara in order to rescue her childhood friend Jennifer from her alcoholism. In the process of regularly spending evenings and sharing wine with Jennifer, Judith becomes dependent on alcohol. In the story's penultimate paragraph, as Judith sits sipping wine alone one evening, she reflects on the move back to Santa Barbara in this way: "I really feel better and better out here, and I think I have never been so happy in my life" (105). Then, in the story's final paragraph, Adams cautions the reader that Judith's solution to her lonely situation in Minnesota may have been an unwise one—that her perceived happiness rests on a foundation of self-deception. Adams's caution comes in a final image in which Judith pets a stray cat who has for the moment allowed her to pet him, but then, "as suddenly as he appeared, with a quick leap out into the dark he is gone" (105).

Perhaps the most atypical story in *After You've Gone,* at least on the surface, is "Favors." It opens with newlyweds, Danny and Phoebe, who have just married after a brief and passionate courtship. Their wedding gift from Danny's best friend, Ralph, has been the "favor" of two weeks at the river house of his architect mother. It was to be "a wonderfully auspicious beginning to their marriage" (108). The first week is a success, but the atmosphere changes with a phone call from Ralph announcing that his mother, Maria, an aging antinuclear protester, has been released from jail. He wonders if Danny and Phoebe would mind if she joins them in her home for the final week of their stay. Her arrival sets up strands of the story that ally it with the other thirteen stories in the volume. There is the possible fragility of the relationship between Danny and Phoebe, of a union whose weak spots are tested by Maria's difficult nature and by the "appalling heat" (118). It is further tested by Maria's fears and insecurities, apparently anchored at least in part in her status as an architect past her prime. The three people coexist uneasily in the house together, their mood finally relieved by a severe thunderstorm, which terrifies Maria and allows her to express her fear of storms to Phoebe, who comforts her. Then, as if signaled by the end of the storm, Ralph arrives, a surprise that relieves them all, Maria and Phoebe especially. "We'll go make sandwiches. . . . We'll celebrate" (122), Phoebe says as she leaves Maria's room. For the moment the problems that have surfaced in the story—problems of potential weakness in the marriage of Danny and Phoebe and of emotional instability of Maria—have been solved by the convenient arrival of a savior, his arrival presumably the second favor in "Favors." However, the restoration of equilibrium in Danny and Phoebe's marriage and in Maria's emotions, like the restoration of so many similarly tentative states of equilibrium in other stories in the collection, seems likely to be a temporary solution. In "Favors" Adams explores the loneliness, uncertainty, and fragility of relationships across generations. She would take the exploration further in her next novel, *Caroline's Daughters* (1991), with particular emphasis on her idea that "it must be worse for people who are much younger."[19]

CHAPTER 6

1990s Novels

Caroline's Daughters, Almost Perfect, A Southern Exposure, and *Medicine Men*

Caroline's Daughters (1991)

By the time of the publication of *Caroline's Daughters* (1991), Adams's first novel of the 1990s, she had published six novels and four story collections, all of them except the first novel, *Careless Love,* widely and, for the most part, positively reviewed. In the process, after the success of *Superior Women* (1984), she had also gained a reputation and the financial security that allowed her greater latitude to explore subjects, themes, settings, and tonal modulations in her fiction with much less concern over whether the result would be a novel or story like those her readers had come to expect. *Caroline's Daughters* is the second novel written to fulfill a two-book contract (*Second Chances* is the first), and it demonstrates that Adams was determined as she entered the 1990s to expand the boundaries of what most readers and critics had come to think of as the "typical" Alice Adams novel.

Caroline's Daughters differs most obviously from Adams's earlier work in a way that she herself describes in an interview: "It's a very moralistic book. . . . I didn't intend it to be anything else," she said. The object of her moralizing was her "disapproval" of the 1980s, including her dislike of Ronald Reagan and of what Adams saw as his perception that "greed is good and conspicuous consumption terrific and rich people are swell"—an ethos that Adams regarded with "enormous disapproval" and loathing.[1] In the subtexts of most of Adams's works before *Caroline's Daughters* there is typically an implied moral code in which the sympathetic main characters privilege values such as self-knowledge, work, romantic idealism, independence, and honesty. Rarely, however, are the works overtly "moralistic" as Adams intended *Caroline's Daughters* to be—and as it turned out, in fact, to be.

In the novel Adams creates powerful social commentary—a profile or portrait of an era in American social and political history. It creates "a microcosm of the 1980s"[2] in which San Francisco becomes not only a character in the novel but also an America in miniature. The large cast of characters represents within certain limits a cross section of 1980s America. Adams focuses the novel on crucial moments in the lives of the five women who are daughters of the title character, Caroline, and her three husbands, two of whom are alive when the story begins. Sage, the oldest daughter, is forty-one in 1985, at the novel's beginning. She is a ceramicist and the daughter of Caroline's first husband, Aaron Levine, who died in World War II. There are also three daughters from Caroline's second marriage, to a doctor, James McAndrew: Liza is thirty-five and a mother, a writer, and the wife of a psychiatrist; Fiona, at thirty-three, is a successful owner of a popular restaurant; and Jill is thirty-one and a wealthy lawyer-stockbroker. Jim McAndrew, their father, is now, like Caroline, in his sixties and deals with his fears of aging by attempting, sometimes with success, to attract younger women. The youngest daughter, Portia, twenty-five and a house sitter, is the only biological child of Caroline and her third husband, Ralph Carter—himself married four times and now in his fifteenth year of a happy marriage to Caroline. In 1985 each daughter's present life has been and continues to be strongly influenced by the culture of the formative years of her childhood, adolescence, and early adulthood, which, as it turns out, has itself been determined at least in part by one of the often-changing phases of her mother's life.

The contrasts among the daughters are so sharply drawn that it is evident that, barely beneath the surface of the narrative, Adams is leading the reader to see the different ways in which the times—the 1980s and the decades leading up to the '80s—have played a role in shaping the character of each of Caroline's daughters. Early in the novel Adams establishes the social and political context by having Caroline and Ralph return to the United States in 1985 after having lived for five years in Portugal. The year of their departure from the United States coincided with the year of Reagan's election to the presidency—the year before he took office for the first of his two terms. The Carters' return to the United States comes a year after Reagan's landslide victory for a second term. By the second page, Caroline's feelings about Fiona and Jill, "these particular daughters, the very rich ones," (4) are shown to be clearly ambivalent. They have come of age in the 1970s, and by 1985, when both are in their early thirties, "Reaganomics" has worked for them: they have both become quite rich, materialistic, and amoral.

The novel's most direct social comment on the 1980s comes through Adams's characterization of Fiona and Jill, those two daughters who have become financially successful in the decade. Fiona has little interest in food or cooking but is nevertheless the owner of Fiona's, a successful and trendy San Francisco restaurant. Her younger sister, Jill, has made a fortune practicing law and playing the stock market—"just under two mil" and, at thirty-one, "just starting out," by her account (55). Also, although she does not need the money, Jill has been led by her greed to participate in what she refers to as "the Game," in which she prostitutes herself to visiting out-of-town businessmen for a thousand dollars a night. Much of Adams's personal distaste for the 1980s is expressed through Fiona and Jill; in the end, both of them seem destined to suffer the consequences of the excesses of the decade. Both will carry their 1980s values into the 1990s, and, whether or not the recession of the early years of the decade will affect them, their morality has been a casualty of the "awful Eighties."

The three other daughters fare much better, perhaps suggesting that their formative years have rendered them less vulnerable to the impulses toward greed and conspicuous consumption that the 1980s had nurtured in Fiona and Jill. All three—Sage, Liza, and Portia—by the end of the novel have moved in the direction of becoming the ideal contemporary women that readers have come to associate with Alice Adams's heroines. Sage has had great success in securing a national reputation for her ceramic figurines and has become financially secure because of it. She is also happily pregnant and looking forward to a life with Stevie, who treats her decently. Liza has realized her dream of becoming a successful professional writer and remains a devoted wife and mother, now free from the most demanding aspects of the duties related to her earlier confining roles. Portia is no longer rootless, having inherited the house of a woman whose house she had cared for. The future of her love life, however, is still unclear since Hilda, her new lover, has accepted a fellowship at the American University in Beirut, a suggestion perhaps that Portia has not yet escaped the consequences of the temporary and artificial euphoria of the 1980s.

Adams's focus on Caroline's five daughters throughout the novel has the effect of diminishing the importance of Caroline's influence on the lives of each daughter, thus affirming the emphasis on "daughters" in the title. Adams provides for Caroline an alternative to a traditional mother role. She has, for example, left Portia to care for herself while still a young woman in her early twenties when Caroline and Ralph went to Portugal for five years; she also keeps what appears to be a definite distance between her and her other daughters, including Liza, with whom she seems most closely to identify. After Ralph

Carter's death, Caroline takes a trip alone to Europe, toying with the idea of a future romantic relationship now that she is, in actuality, free of familial obligations. There is even a fantasy almost realized of an affair with Roland Gallo, the San Francisco politico who had broken the heart of Sage and who had had an affair with Fiona.

Finally, the reader observes Caroline as she imagines alternatives for her own life, placing the burden of the direction her children's lives have taken (and will take in the future) on the social mores of the decade—the era—in which they developed during their formative years. In the final pages of the novel, Caroline tracks down the sister of a woman she once knew who fell on hard times and whose image has haunted her for quite a while. When she meets with Mavis Higgins, the sister, Mavis makes this remark: "We'll all be better once the awful Eighties are over" (306). Caroline agrees and "hopes that the Nineties . . . will be a vast improvement" (307). Beyond emphasizing the importance of an era's culture for the development of one's character—especially during one's formative years—Adams presents in *Caroline's Daughters* a vision of the Alice Adams woman, now a mother in her sixties, in which a mother provides a living example of the ideal contemporary woman. The role of mothers as represented in the novel is to allow their daughters to live their lives relatively free from interference from their mothers. From beginning to end Caroline is a self-reliant woman who never forfeits her own need for independence, and through her Adams offers a universal statement about motherhood that transcends her visceral distaste for the 1980s.

Almost Perfect (1993)

With her eighth novel, *Almost Perfect,* Adams retained the setting of the San Francisco of the "awful Eighties" that had provided the setting for *Caroline's Daughters,* but in *Almost Perfect* she abandoned what she had called her "moralistic" perspective and created two of her most memorable characters as well as what is perhaps her most powerful love story. In it, Stella Blake, a bright, attractive, and successful half-Mexican reporter, has an intense attraction over a two-year period to the magnetic, handsome, and dangerously volatile commercial artist Richard Fallon. Stella's attraction to Richard is founded on tangible, shared qualities that give their love substance. Both are talented and intelligent (Richard is often described as brilliant; Stella is a bright, gifted writer); both are physically attractive and drawn to each other sexually (in Richard's saner moments the attraction is mutual; in her saner moments Stella questions how she can possibly be so physically drawn to Richard and not be crazy); and neither is at the time in a permanent relationship with another person (though Richard has two former wives who come in and out of his life; Stella has in her past only a long-ago love for a much older movie star, Liam O'Gara, who comes in and out of her mind).

In the eyes of much of the outside world—and to each other for much of the time—Richard and Stella seem almost perfect together. As it turns out, though, there persists until near the end of the novel a power imbalance in their relationship that consistently favors Richard, and he uses that power over and over again to keep Stella in a position of emotional dependence on him. Richard derives his power from his masculine charm, his charisma; from his unpredictability; and from his perception and presumption of the privilege that comes from the fact that he does, in fact, have a talent for interior design that sets him apart from others. He consistently uses this power to manipulate others—to create in them the illusion that he is indispensible to them.

Adams, through her handling of her favored third-person, omniscient point of view with a narrative focus that shifts mainly between Stella and Richard, often signaled by chapter headings telling whose chapter it is, allows the reader from the beginning to glimpse forces operating beneath the surface of the relationship that give it a mythic quality and also warn of the potential for tragedy in it—especially for Richard—and for triumph—most likely for Stella, though this is never certain until the end. The most revealing moment in Stella's attraction to Richard comes early in their relationship when they argue after returning from dinner with two of Richard's friends. As Richard is about to leave Stella in a fury, she has a sensation of panic: "A huge bird caged in her chest beats its wings against her ribs. Insufferable. She cannot let him go" (65). This is a Yeatsian moment, one that seems as if it could have come from "Leda and the Swan." It is as if Richard, disguised as a perfect man, has entered Stella—has raped her soul—as Zeus entered Leda—raped her—disguised as a swan, and she has no ability to cast him or his seed out. Leda can only wonder if she can internalize some of Zeus's power before he leaves her forever. And Stella, like Leda, can only wonder whether she will be able to internalize Richard's knowledge —his genius—before he turns her loose, as he manipulatively threatens to do on many occasions throughout their relationship and as he eventually does for a man with whom he has flirted throughout the novel. Ironically Richard leaves Stella no babies—no Helens and no Clytemnestras, as Zeus leaves Leda—but he does leave her a cat named Eve, named diabolically for an off-and-on mistress, Eva.

As Stella continually questions her motives for loving Richard, to herself as well as, occasionally, to her friends and to the reader, and as she experiences the passion and panic that go with loving him, Richard is demonstrating the wild swings that his personality goes through, sometimes from moment to moment, sometimes from hour to hour, swings that he often uses to control others, Stella most dramatically. He is capable at one moment of showering her with love, with compliments, and with gifts of wine and food, often sharing the cooking with her. He even brings her juice in bed in the mornings and convinces her he doesn't want ever to leave their "enchanted cottage" and go out to be with friends (63). However, following intimate moments and close times together, Richard engages in a stream of thoughts regarding Stella that often reveal a dark, cruel side and betray his real feelings about her, feelings that allow him to place himself in a position of power over her: he considers her "an exceptionally nice woman, intelligent (maybe a little too intelligent?) and kind. And not pretty or beautiful. . . . [Her] wide flat mouth is so vulnerable (too vulnerable?) taking him in" (71). In one particular series of episodes during which Richard reveals to the reader his egomania, Stella calls his studio to say that her father has died and that she needs Richard to be with her. He listens to her pleading on his voice-mail machine and refuses to pick up the phone, unwilling to go to Stella when she badly needs him. Instead, he waits at the studio for an appointment that, as it turns out, is with a woman who becomes his off-and-on mistress. This is Eva, "a woman so tall and beautiful" that Richard immediately goes to bed with her during their first meeting, the day of Stella's father's death and just after her call to Richard for moral support. Finally, that evening, on his way to comfort Stella, he buys her the cat mentioned earlier, sadistically naming the cat Eve, after Eva, the woman he has taken to bed earlier that day. Ironically, and without Stella's being aware of the irony, he has left Stella with a symbol of his ability to replace her with another woman when it pleases him.

The novel moves back and forth between episodes in which Richard is on his best behavior and those in which he is at his worst, as he treats Stella with tenderness one moment and with contempt the next. Finally, however, Stella is unable to reconcile this loving Richard with the many other Richards, one of whom becomes at times a "raging furious stranger," a terrifying drunk (116) whose unpredictability gives him power that robs Stella of her independence and undermines her self-esteem. His destructiveness and his self-destructiveness coupled with Stella's increased success as a writer finally drain Richard of his power and bring about the disintegration of their relationship, at last allowing Stella to begin a life that becomes increasingly rewarding, free, and richly self-fulfilling. For his part, Richard becomes, more often than not, completely irrational. His financial situation, never solid, becomes hopeless when the moneyed backer of his main business enterprise commits suicide; Richard is forced to borrow money from Stella, one of many acts that drive him to leave Stella and instruct her not to try to locate him. Finally when he is very close to the point of ending his life, he backs out of suicide and instead establishes a serious relationship with his longtime gay friend Andrew. The two are together when the reader last sees them at a clinic in Mexico where Andrew will be treated for AIDS and where Richard will be tested, he thinks, and perhaps take the cure "prophylactically" (235). Seemingly somewhat delusional at this point and as ever egomaniacal, Richard recalls his life with Stella, concluding, "I never was so beautiful as I was with Stella." Perhaps one day he will go back to her, he thinks (235), indicating that even in his lowest moment in the novel he refuses to relinquish the illusion of actual power that he labored under for the two years of his relationship with Stella.

Not knowing for some time whether Richard is dead or alive, Stella is at first haunted by thoughts of him; then she finally makes peace with her memories of the two years they were together. In the end, as a nationally known, financially independent writer with articles in the best national magazines, she decides to rent an office for her writing in a downtown building, a place where she can move forward with her life: "In this room, God knows, where Richard has never been, and where the version of herself who loved and lived with Richard has not been either, Stella does not think of him. She works, and she is slowly aware of the emergence within herself of a saner, stronger person" (232).

Stella has arrived at this point of becoming perhaps Adams's strongest and most fully individuated character by no accident. Her self-knowledge has come from hard work, deep reflection, and a willingness to be vulnerable. These are all qualities that Adams's strong women exhibit, none perhaps reaching the level of success in professional terms or in self-knowledge that Stella achieves at the end of *Almost Perfect*. Even at the novel's conclusion, when she is celebrating her autonomy, her recent fame as a writer, and her independence from Richard, Stella reveals in an interview with her friend Justine that she remains open to the mystery of romantic love. As she tells Justine, however, when she thinks of the words "in love" "it has less and less to do with the actual Richard Fallon" (243) and more to do with the capacity to remain open to another human being—and to do so even when there is a risk of pain. Adams's strong women work to achieve this level of openness and a belief in the possibility that romantic love exists while also keeping intact a strong sense of self. Stella demonstrates her openness in her willingness to "try again" at the conclusion of the novel in her relationship with John Schmidt, a man capable of seeing Stella as an equal. It is no coincidence, of course, that Adams closes her fictional treatment of the 1980s, the decade in which she ended her long relationship with Bob McNie, on whom Richard Fallon is partially patterned, with the parting of Stella and Richard. By 1993, the year of publication of *Almost Perfect,* Adams had been in a relationship with Dr. Daniel Simon, who would play a significant role in the events out of which her 1997 novel, *Medicine Men,* grew.

A Southern Exposure (1995)

For her primary physical setting in *A Southern Exposure* (1995), Adams returned to the place that played such an important role in her life and in her fiction, a small North Carolina town she calls Pinehill. It is a town very close geographically to her fictional Hilton, a thinly disguised Chapel Hill, as the reader learns when Sally Jane ("Brett") Byrd, wife of the famous local poet and a central character in *A Southern Exposure,* reveals that she "was the university president's daughter over in Hilton" (13). Occasional character types in the novel are recognizable from earlier Hilton stories. However, none of the specific characters are carried over from the early stories, and it is clear from the beginning that Adams is attempting several ambitious things in *A Southern Exposure* that she has not tried before. The novel takes place in the relatively limited time period of 1939–1944, a time, in one reviewer's words, "when people's lives were determined by their gender, their religion, and the color of their skin."[3] Adams creates two characters, Cynthia Baird and her daughter, Abby, who are ahead of their time and who in this pre-feminist, pre–civil rights era make enormous strides toward becoming the kind of free-spirited, autonomous, politically progressive women who gained their independence in Adams's earlier novels, though typically in works before *A Southern Exposure* they had done it in decades that came after the 1940s.

At first glance Cynthia Baird seems an unlikely one to challenge the rigid social and gender constructs of the late 1930s and early 1940s, particularly those of the South; her family—her eleven-year-old daughter, Abby, her husband, Harry, and herself—seems an odd group to break into the upper levels of polite society in a small Southern town just beyond the fringes of a university campus—a Southern town with clearly defined, elitist ideas regarding "social class." The Bairds do not appear to be likely prospects at the beginning of the novel to challenge from within those class constructions of the town toward which they are heading and in which they will soon settle; clearly it appears unlikely that they could successfully challenge long-held Southern biases related to race and ethnicity. As the novel opens, the Bairds are traveling south with little money, riding in an older, once-grand, wood-paneled station wagon that signals their faded hopes of gaining upward social mobility in Connecticut. Each member of the family is escaping something left behind as the family heads toward a new start in the South. Cynthia is leaving behind an outstanding bill at Lord & Taylor's as well as an almost-consummated illicit love affair. Harry is escaping a boring position as a country club manager as well as a life of too much drinking and too many extramarital flirtations that went too far. The daughter, Abby, is leaving the snobbish private school where she felt herself an outsider—a school in which her only true friend was Benny, the bright and talented African American son of the school's janitor. As Harry thinks of it during their trip South, "In the pristine, uncharted region [of Pinehill] he and Cynthia will regain their innocence; once more they will be in love and rich again, as before the Crash, now almost ten years back, when Cynthia's golden money [apparently inherited] seemed an endless stream" (4).

What follows the arrival of the Bairds in Pinehill is a nuanced representation of life in a small Southern town in the years leading up to the beginning (and finally near the end) of World War II, an intriguing portrait of a quaint mid-Southern town in the years before and during the war. The novel provides penetrating social satire and abundant evidence of human foibles in its complex characterizations of the inhabitants of Pinehill, their interactions, and the social institutions that form the backdrop for the novel's interwoven story lines. Pinehill's culture appears guided by the men, who take charge of sustaining the town's order and direction in the public sphere. Russell Byrd is, initially at least, the town's pride and joy—its local attraction. He is known far and wide as the town's famous writer, a community anchor who has married the daughter of the nearby university's former president and fathered five children by her.

Granted, Russ will in the course of the novel respond to Brett's emotional difficulties with great insensitivity by turning her over to another man, a psychiatrist who will finally bring about her accidental death by administering a shock treatment in his nearby sanitarium for mental patients. And Russ will finally, after Brett's death, marry Deirdre, a former mistress and the mother of his son; he will also have a second child by her, a fact that seems not to diminish the town's affection for him. Because of his writing and his reputation, Russ has also attracted to the town, without intending to, Jimmy Hightower, whose wealthy wife has provided the money necessary to build a house close to Jimmy's idolized, hoped-for mentor, Russ. But Jimmy also has assumed the role of tour guide and informal historian for those, like Cynthia, who wish to learn more about the town. For his part, Harry, quickly on the heels of the Bairds' arrival in Pinehill, becomes the garrulous family spokesman who flatters the decorator of their temporary suite at the local Colonial Inn and thereby insinuates the Bairds into the town's social world. The men, then, direct the town's narrative in the public sphere, though curiously none of them, including Harry, seem actually to earn money by working at a job—at least not until Jimmy writes a best-selling novel and Harry moves to Washington for a bureaucratic governmental position.

The women inhabit the domestic sphere behind the scenes, following their traditional feminine roles. They decorate; they talk of clothes and food; and they pass back and forth among themselves rumors about one another, as well as about those on the periphery of their social world. As in most small towns, there is much to gossip about. Early on, when the Bairds arrive, there are whisperings about Cynthia's black dress as being "northern" and inappropriate for the season. There is the true story of Russ Byrd's affair with Deirdre Yates, by whom he has an illegitimate son, a story that Cynthia actually learns about from Jimmy Hightower on one of their tours of the town. By the time Jimmy recounts it to Cynthia, it is a story that has already been accepted as a fact by most of Pinehill's residents. There is a story, also true, of Dorothy Bigelow's affair with Clifton Lee, husband of her friend Irene. In addition, there is a rumor about Brett's "crush" on her psychiatrist, Dr. Clyde Drake, who comes often to visit the Byrds after Brett is released from the sanitarium after her first stay and before she returns for the shock treatments that will kill her. Later, Drake brings with him his wife, Norris, who, it is rumored (accurately), is having a sexual affair with Russ Byrd. These stories, many chronicling events that actually occur in Pinehill and some embellished or entirely untrue, provide the narrative thread that serves to unify the town. They also provide the thread of narrative that makes *A Southern Exposure* excellent social satire.

The novel often goes beyond the satirical, however, in its pointed probing and politically nuanced study of gender constructions and racial and ethnic dynamics in the era immediately preceding the feminist and civil rights revolutions that would take place in the late 1950s and 1960s. Adams's novel brings the conflicts that resulted from those constructions and those dynamics into sharp focus in *A Southern Exposure* and makes the case for change in an overtly didactic rather than satirical way. At heart, the novel is a chronicle of the evolution of Cynthia Baird from her state of relative powerlessness in a patriarchal world to one in which she is a highly conscious, autonomous individual who has rejected the socially constructed role she has been assigned as a woman, a powerlessness that increasingly gives her empathy for those who are oppressed or marginalized. Ultimately this empowers her, prompting her to finish college and apply to law school. Other events strengthen Cynthia's growing social consciousness during her first months in Pinehill, among them her discovery of Esther Hightower's feelings of being marginalized by her Jewishness in this WASP society, so much so that she is tearful and frightened at the thought of appearing downstairs among the guests at a party given by her and her husband, Jimmy.

The true turning point in the development of Cynthia's independence and of her social consciousness comes when Harry accepts work in Washington, thus leaving Cynthia on her own with Abby in Pinehill. At this point she contemplates what it would be like to be completely free of Harry, and, in spite of often feeling lonely and sexually unfulfilled without Harry, she begins to savor her autonomy. She even has a long-dreamed-of sexual affair with Russ Byrd, whose proposal of marriage she turns down because neither honestly wants the marriage. When she leaves Pinehill to rejoin Harry in their marriage in Washington, she decides to pursue her college education, ultimately taking her degree and applying to law school. In her newfound freedom, she decides to return to Pinehill, for which she has developed profound affection. She buys and restores the historically significant but rundown house once occupied by Deirdre with plans to use it as a second home for the Baird family—for what one Pinehill resident refers to ironically as their pied-à-terre. The novel ends with a party celebrating Cynthia's success.

As Cynthia has been undergoing her transformation, Abby, almost on her own and with little interference or help from Harry or Cynthia, has been developing a strong social awareness during those impressionable years of eleven to sixteen, the early years of which have been spent in racist Pinehill. She has brought with her from Connecticut to Pinehill at the age eleven a much more open attitude in matters of race than her peers and their parents in Pineville have. Through her time in Pinehill she carries on a correspondence with her African American friend Benny in Connecticut, and she entertains thoughts of having him visit her in Pinehill, though she is sadly aware of the racist resistance that he would face if he should come: Pinehill residents would think of Benny as "colored" and would treat him shabbily. At a later point she contemplates what kissing Benny would be like. When she moves with Cynthia to Washington, she sends back to her friend in Pinehill a paper she has written condemning racial prejudice and making a case for racial equality. Her "radical" ideas spread quickly through the gossip channels of Pinehill, and Harry begins to refer to the essay as her "Infamous Integration Paper" (281), a paper that prompted general disapproval among the parents of her Pinehill friends. When the Bairds return for Russ and Deirdre's wedding, however, her relationships with her friends, particularly her best friend, Betsy Lee, have not been altered. The reader is left with the impression that the town itself is growing, if not progressive, at least more tolerant of the differences between people of different social positions.

Adams goes into new territory with *A Southern Exposure,* and she does it by a kind of sleight of hand. Cynthia seems at first glance to be a liberated Alice Adams woman in the direct line of those like Louisa Calloway in *Families and Survivors,* Daphne Matthiesen in *Rich Rewards,* or Megan Greene in *Superior Women*. But Cynthia is actually of a generation earlier than most of Adams's earlier main characters. Hers is the generation that preceded these women. Megan, for example, was born in 1926; Louisa was born in 1927. Cynthia, by contrast, was born in 1907. It is Abby, born in 1928, who is closer generationally to those earlier Adams women (and to Adams herself). They, for the most part, have become and are becoming liberated in a later era than Cynthia. In *A Southern Exposure* Adams has demonstrated that the radical progressive changes that came with the civil rights and women's rights movements of the 1950s and 1960s were a long time in the making, as Cynthia realizes they would be. Abby and those in her generation who think similarly offer the promise that the hope for progress in the realm of racial and gender equality is real. In *After the War* (2000), Adams's posthumously published sequel to *A Southern Exposure,* she would examine the degree to which Abby's generation was poised to carry this hope forward after war has ended.

Medicine Men (1997)

The publication of *Medicine Men* immediately followed the 1995 release of *A Southern Exposure,* and in an interview after publication of the latter Adams acknowledged she had started writing that novel "at a time I wasn't feeling too great and I wanted to get somewhere else"; "so," in her words, "I really did get somewhere else, which is to say North Carolina in the 1930s."[4] The reference to not "feeling too great" was a reference to her painful bout with cancer, for which she was successfully treated in 1992 (just before publication of *Almost Perfect*) and for which she received a clean bill of health in late 1994, ten months before the publication of *A Southern Exposure.* As early as 1993 Adams had begun to deal in print with her illness and the treatment associated with it, and her thoughts about the illness ultimately evolved into her next novel, *Medicine Men.* She first drew on her experiences "fictionally" in an essay/story, "A Shadow on the Brain," which was published as nonfiction in *Allure* in September 1993. At the end of the piece *Allure* noted, "Names and some circumstances in this piece have been changed by the author to protect the people close to her."[5] Adams denied that she knew of this disclaimer or that the piece would be presented as nonfiction, and she later revised parts of the *Allure* piece and included them in *Medicine Men,* clearly marked as "a novel" on the book's dust jacket and on its title page as "a novel by Alice Adams." In the *Allure* essay/story the first-person narrator undergoes an endoscopic treatment, surgery, and then radiation similar to the treatment undergone by Molly Bonner, the main character in *Medicine Men*—and similar to the illness and surgery that Adams went through in 1992. The line separating fact and fiction in this case becomes a very thin one.

A majority of the reviewers—and they were overwhelmingly positive about the novel—resisted making reference to Adams's own illness, and when they did refer to it, the references were made briefly and in passing. One reviewer characterized the effect of Adams's accomplishment in *Medicine Men* by alluding to the ancient Greek myth of Asclepius,[6] who was thought to be a doctor of extraordinary skill. Some considered him to be godlike in his abilities to heal, even to bring the dead back to life. Eventually Asclepius began to believe he was a god and thus angered Zeus, who struck him dead with a thunderbolt. Adams plays the role of Zeus in *Medicine Men,* striking those doctors who most egregiously abuse their power both in medical settings and out of them with verbal thunderbolts.

In an interview shortly before the release of *Medicine Men,* Adams said this of the book: "I like the title quite a lot. . . . It's about doctors . . . it's mean and angry."[7] And there is no denying that the novel's satire, which comes through Adams's favorite omniscient-author point of view with a narrative focus that is largely on Molly but one that shifts among several of the characters, is aimed squarely at the medical establishment. Adams handles the "mean and angry" direct attacks on irresponsible medical practices that take place over the course of the novel obliquely by structuring them around the "romantic" relationships of Molly Bonner and her best friend, Felicia Flood, with medicine men—Molly's with Dr. Dave Jacobs and her best friend's with Dr. Raleigh ("Sandy") Sanderson—whose malpractice is less medical than psychological. On the face of it, Jacobs, who has recently lost his wife, has only Molly's best interests at heart. He meets her at Felicia's party in the novel's first chapter and immediately insists on taking her home when she suffers a nosebleed, arguing that, in his medical opinion, she should perhaps consult a specialist.

As it turns out, Molly has a malignant tumor the size of a golf ball located in her sinuses, and many of the novel's dramatic "events" from the point of this discovery chronicle the stages in her treatment and mistreatment until she ultimately becomes free of the tumor. Also in the process she becomes free of Jacobs, who has insinuated himself into every stage of Molly's treatment and who has arguably been instrumental in bringing about her cure. But from the beginning Molly has resisted his attempts to control her by taking away her choices of the types of treatments she might pursue and the doctors who would be in charge of administering them. All the while he has drawn her, mostly against her will, into a sexual relationship even in the face of her protests that she does not want such a relationship with him. Eventually she does have sex with him, but, as she tells Felicia at the very beginning of Jacobs's romantic pursuit of her, "I wasn't exactly attracted to him" (42). And by the end of her treatments, all engineered by Jacobs on the strength of his medical expertise, she is triumphant in declaring her independence from him and resisting his further intrusion into her life: "Dave, you have to go now. I'm tired. I don't want to see you. . . . I'm through. . . . Dave, good-bye" (205). She has sensed all along that Jacobs's need to exert his power has been a driving force in his involvement in her treatment, and he has used the power of his position as a knowledgeable medicine man to form a personal relationship with Molly. All along she has tried to resist giving him power over her, and in the end, as she tells him goodbye, she regains her autonomy and her independence from him as she regains her health and her freedom from the medical condition that brought them together in the first place.

Like Molly's relationship with Jacobs, Felicia's relationship with the famous heart surgeon Dr. Raleigh ("Sandy") Sanderson is not one of doctor and patient; neither does it involve medical abuse or malpractice, but it does involve an overt form of psychological abuse that turns, in the end, into physical abuse. Sanderson's egomania is evident from the beginning. Early in the novel Adams presents him through close omniscient narration in which he reveals himself to be a married man who is proud of his sexual prowess and of his good fortune in being able to have sex with his operating room nurses while also having a mistress. He has met Molly's friend Felicia sometime before the novel opens, and even after they became lovers he continued his habit of going to bed with his nurses. He justifies this by noting that the heart surgery operations he performs thrill him: "Small wonder, then, that after such an exciting, deeply felt triumph he should feel himself excited in a sexual way." (17). This routinely leads him into sexual relationships immediately after performing surgery with one or the other of his nurses. His expertise in the operating room appears to give him power over his nurses outside it. He doesn't consider these acts to constitute infidelity to Felicia, his mistress, or to his wife, Connie, a recovering alcoholic whose self-confidence has long ago apparently been shattered at least in part by Sanderson's treatment of her. Eventually, much to her credit, she will regain her autonomy and leave him.

Adams, then, constructs the novel around the movement of the two women, Molly and Felicia, first toward dependence on and then escape from their reliance on the two men, Jacobs and Sanderson, both of whom have power that resides principally in their position in the medical establishment. Molly eventually escapes Jacobs when he becomes so overbearing and insistent on his infallibility that she dismisses him from her life; Felicia escapes Sanderson after he strikes her in a fit of jealousy sparked by her interest in another man. The punishment for the benignly manipulative Jacobs is exile from the life of Molly, who becomes the healed and autonomous Adams female. For Sanderson, who has conferred on himself godlike status and mercilessly abused his power, Adams has a special thunderbolt that will be revealed at the end of the novel. Meanwhile, the two-relationship structure forms a frame for the episodic narrative, many episodes of which deal with Molly's encounters with various medicine men other than Jacobs—doctors by whom she is seen professionally in the course of her treatment for the cancerous growth in her sinuses.

From the beginning of her entry into the medical world of specialists who are ostensibly committed to treating her illness until the time she is finally free of the medical procedures and the cancer itself, Molly has experiences that are at once frighteningly real and comically surreal, tinged with gallows humor. It is through Molly's journey from nosebleeds to cure at the hands of often careless egotists like the ear, nose, and throat specialist Dr. Beckle and Dr. Stinger, a careless surgeon, that Adams's "mean and angry" criticism of the medical establishment is sharpest and most effective. When Adams's lawyer worried that she might be sued by doctors who recognized themselves in the fictional doctors in *Medicine Men* (many drawn from Adams's experiences during her own treatment), she "told him not to worry. I can always sue them in return for malpractice."[8]

All of Adams's "mean and angry" criticisms of the medical establishment are made abundantly clear in the episodic part of the novel dealing with Molly and her illness, but Adams also makes it clear that, at least in the world of this novel, there is a system of checks and balances in the medical establishment that often serves to negatively reinforce or punish the irresponsible practitioners in the medical world when they cross the line into malpractice. The reader does not learn how the checks and balances may work eventually to change the behavior of those irresponsible practitioners or to create hospital environments that are less dehumanizing for patients, who are stripped of their dignity as they wait in long lines to be called in, often by the wrong name, for treatment, only to be greeted by impersonal hospital staff, and who wonder, "What terrible thing have I done to be brought so low, to this place of punishment and pain?" (125). Adams perhaps wishes that readers of her novel may be moved to hasten positive action that will effect needed changes. In any event, Adams's representation of these situations and conditions in the sphere of inhumane medical treatment turn her social satire into didactic social criticism.

Interestingly, Adams's most withering criticism is reserved for surgeon Sandy Sanderson, the most egotistical of the doctors in the novel and Felicia's former lover, whose main transgressions, as far as the reader knows, do not fall into the category of missed diagnoses or medical malpractice. Adams faults him for other things that may allow the reader to better understand *Medicine Men* in the context of her other works. Adams devotes several full chapters and parts of others to Sandy's stream-of-consciousness thoughts and to his behavior. In the first of these he justifies his sexual behavior, including his infidelity to his wife and mistress; in another he is shown actually striking Felicia in anger out of his jealousy; in yet another he becomes angry at a patient for describing his prostate problems. Sandy's anger comes from his fears of his own medical difficulties. Now, like many doctors in the novel, he is "swollen with self-importance and self-deception" (165); and in the final chapter (devoted entirely to Sandy's thoughts and actions) the reader sees him at his nastiest, least understanding, most pessimistic self. In this chapter he is at the Alta Linda hospital, where Molly received her final radiation treatment before going AWOL. In his self-deception bordering on delusion, Sandy denies his own need for radiation for his prostate tumor and imagines how he will gain power investing in the hospital's radiation equipment. The final sentences of the novel contain his final thoughts, and they seem to suggest that, in the end, he has come to understand his plight, though likely too late to do anything about it: "This is the worst place I've ever been. This is hell" (239).

By this point the reader realizes that Adams's ideas related to power struggles in relationships of the kind represented in *Medicine Men* are by no means restricted to those within the medical establishment. In virtually all of Adams's work, relationships in which power valences are badly out of balance between individuals—relationships in which one person is denied freedom and autonomy so that another can have power—are doomed to fail. Adams's strongest characters, most often her strong women, invariably resist imprisonment in unequal relationships. Those who refuse to relinquish their power over another person in a relationship—those who refuse to give up the delusion that they are godlike—will quite likely be doomed in Adams's novels and stories to a fate akin to that of Asclepius: they will be struck with a thunderbolt of one sort or another.

CHAPTER 7

1990s Stories

The Last Lovely City

In the 1990s Adams published four novels—one every two years beginning in 1991. During the decade she also wrote and published more than two dozen short stories, and in 1999 she collected thirteen of her stories—most of which had originally appeared in the 1990s—in *The Last Lovely City* (1999), her final short story collection and the last book Adams would publish during her lifetime. As was true for all of Adams's fourteen previous fictional volumes except her first, *Careless Love*—ten novels and four short story collections—*The Last Lovely City* was widely and, for the most part, favorably reviewed. Many of the reviewers were acquainted with Adams's earlier works and pointed to her established reputation as a master of the short story form, some underlining the fact that five of the volume's thirteen stories had first appeared in the *New Yorker,* and some reminding readers that from the beginning, her novels and stories, like those in the present volume, had dealt with the complexity of relationships, with the hope of finding love, and with the importance of meaningful work in the quest for autonomy—particularly for women in a patriarchal society.

As has been true of earlier Adams story collections, the title story of *The Last Lovely City* provides a window into the heart of many stories in the volume—in this case especially into the volume's Part One, which contains the first nine stories. Part Two contains four stories loosely connected and constituting a novella of sorts. The title story, "The Last Lovely City," appeared in the *New Yorker* in 1991 and was the earliest of the previously published stories contained in Part One. It is also the richest story in *The Last Lovely City*—the volume's masterpiece—and it helps provide context for the seven stories that precede it in the collection, as well as the one that follows it as the last story in the first part of the collection. In September 1990—the present time of the story—Benito Zamora, a famous cardiologist and the main character of "The Last Lovely City," is walking alone on the sands of Stinson Beach outside San Francisco toward the Golden Gate. He knows that if he continues in his southward direction "he will [soon] be in sight of beautiful, mystical San Francisco, the city and the center of all his early dreams, the city where everything, finally, happened" (100). Much has happened in the fifty years between his early dreams before he came to San Francisco and the present: Zamora finished medical school at Stanford and married a wonderful woman, Elizabeth Montague (many notches above him on the social scale and now, in 1990, recently deceased); then he became a famous cardiologist, made a fortune in real estate, and funded two free clinics back in Chiapas, Mexico, near his childhood home in Oaxaca, where his mother still lives.

Walking on the sand of Stinson Beach in the story's present, Zamora has slipped away from a party, some of whose attendees are reminders of a time before he was the rich, famous cardiologist nicknamed Dr. Do-Good, "an epithet replete with irony, and one that he much dislikes" (89). One of those attendees is a notoriously corrupt lawyer, Herman Tolliver, who at an early stage of Zamora's career had involved Zamora in a series of shady real estate deals that made him a huge fortune; a second is a now-wealthy, many-times-married Mexican woman, Dolores Gutierrez, with whom Zamora had carried on a sexual affair before he met his wife, Elizabeth. Carla, a young newspaper reporter he had met a month before at a dinner, has brought Zamora to this party, for reasons he can only imagine: perhaps she wishes to interview him, he thinks, or, as his imagination takes over, there is the unlikely possibility that she is romantically interested in him. Zamora contemplates all of these things and more on his walk: his early idealistic dreams of the good life he would lead as a San Francisco doctor; his missteps with Dolores Gutierrez, who shamefully, as some kind of joke that involved their shared status as Mexican immigrants, asked him to pay her after a sexual encounter; his corruption by the shady real estate deals with Tolliver; the death of his beloved Elizabeth and the loneliness that he continues to feel without her; his fantasy of a romantic relationship with the youthful and exciting Carla, who might be interested in beginning a life with him. He fantasizes that she will completely rejuvenate his beautiful house with its breathtaking views of the water and of San Francisco. In his imagination he can see freshly from that house what he thinks of as the "tall, pale city, lovely and unreal," and he longingly remembers his "amazement at that city, years back, when he roamed its streets as an almost indigent medical student" (95).

With Zamora's story—with his memories of what has been and his fantasies about what might yet be—Adams comes as close as she has since

Beautiful Girl to embracing and extending the tradition of Romantic idealism, particularly as it has come down through Fitzgerald. Zamora's reflections on the "beautiful, mystical San Francisco, the city and the center of all his early dreams," call to mind the scene at the end of *The Great Gatsby* in which Nick Carraway imagines what it must have been like for the Dutch sailors when they first set eyes on the new world: "For a transitory enchanted moment man must have held his breath in the presence of this continent, compelled into an aesthetic contemplation he neither understood nor desired, face to face for the last time in history with something commensurate to his capacity for wonder."[1] Zamora first sees San Francisco in much the same way that Nick imagines the Dutch sailors saw that "fresh green breast of the new world"[2]—as an unspoiled place of infinite possibilities. The wasteland in *Gatsby,* of course, spreads west, spoiling the "green breast of the new world" as it moves from the East Coast toward the West. Adams extends the metaphor all the way to the West Coast and San Francisco: the last lovely city—far west of Gatsby's West Egg—becomes corrupted. For Adams at the level of the larger story that is, if only symbolically, related to *Gatsby,* the metaphor works on an East/West axis, but it operates for Zamora and his story on a North/South one. San Francisco was lovely for him on a personal level as he saw it coming up from Mexico. Then his shady dealings with the lawyer Tolliver became one of the early forces that helped Zamora corrupt San Francisco for himself, even as the widespread corruption was spoiling the last lovely city for so many others.

As Zamora reflects on his past dreams, his loss of those dreams through his own greed, and the possibility of reclaiming, perhaps through Carla, that sense of wonder that he once had, Carla runs up from behind. She has chased him in the sand, and when she catches him he feels "a strange, warm quiet excitement" (101) as they walk south, not yet in sight of the "pale and distant and invisible" city. His dreams of a life with Carla, though, are short lived, as she informs him on their walk together that she is engaged to the son of the party's hostess. They reach a wall of high rocks, which obscures any chance of a view of San Francisco, the sun sinks into the ocean, and "Benito's heart has sunk with it" (103). At the wall they turn around and head back in the direction of the party. Zamora quickly rebounds from the disappointment of Carla's news with an alternate plan and informs her that he will move back to Mexico permanently and involve himself in work with the poor who are patients in the hospitals that he funds.

Of central importance in this story is the cyclical way that dreams and disenchantment have operated throughout Zamora's life. He had apparently not been especially conscious of this pattern until the day of the party and of his walk on the beach, during which he comes to understand more about the plight of the idealist in a modern materialistic society. When he came to America he dreamed of going to Stanford and becoming a doctor. His "amazement at the city"—his dream of what it seemed to promise to an "almost indigent medical student"—came early on to be tainted by a desire to own it: "He wanted the city, both to possess and to immerse himself in it" (95). On the day of his Stinson Beach walk he comes to see that his "greed" had led him to the real estate deal with Tolliver, to his own part in the corruption of the last lovely city, and to the compromising of his ideals as well: he had idealized San Francisco and then proceeded, almost unthinkingly, to corrupt it. His guilt over this is, in retrospect, enormous, and it appears to be the single most important instance in which he has compromised his ideals. He also idealized Elizabeth Montague—whose social credentials made her the golden girl for a poor Mexican immigrant—and married her, and from all signs in the story the two had an extraordinary relationship. When he lost Elizabeth, he continued to mourn her loss, but this does not prevent him from idealistically envisioning a relationship with Carla. However, when that fleeting fantasy of life with Carla proves futile, he, almost reflexively, makes a quick decision: he will return to the place of his youth to care for his aging mother and to work in those hospitals that had been born, the reader assumes, out of his idealistic wish to help the poor in his home country.

The story's ending is left open, and the reader has no way of knowing whether Zamora seriously intends to return to Mexico, though after speaking of it as a plan to Carla he feels "committed to this action." His thoughts about the prospect are tinged with sadness when he considers the possibility that he "will work in his clinics, with his own poor" for "as long as he lasts" (103). What the reader knows about Zamora, though, from past actions is that his capacity to hope and dream is enduring. True, he has compromised his ideals as he did in entering into the business deals with Tolliver in order to "own" part of his idealized San Francisco, but, as Carla reminds him, he was then able as a consequence to fulfill a dream of funding clinics in Mexico. He idealized Elizabeth, in part because of her impeccable social credentials that were so important to an "almost indigent medical student." He then went on to spend years of happiness with her, building a relationship that transcended considerations of social status. Now that she is gone, Zamora has not given up on love, as his fantasies about a life with Carla demonstrate. Adams appears not to judge Zamora for the times he has compromised his dreams or for those times when he has given in to moments of sadness or despair; she seems rather to applaud his willingness to embrace new dreams after the society that makes ownership sacred and owners seem godlike has lured him into compromising his ideals. He is a dreamer who at first idealized Elizabeth in part for her social status but then took her off the pedestal and loved her apart from her value as a commodity.

Other stories in the first part of *The Last Lovely City* contain representations of the pattern of idealization, disenchantment, and then the restoration of hope that is present in Zamora's story. They often stress the resiliency—the willingness to "try again," similar to Zamora's, though not in quite such elaborate detail as in his story—of the main character's capacity for optimism and renewal of idealism after early dreams or initial attractions have faded or failed. In the case of "Old Love Affairs" Adams emphasizes the resiliency of the romantic impulse in a dramatic, perhaps exaggerated, way. The main character, Lucretia Baine (a reporter like Carla from "The Last Lovely City," though a generation older), has been married three times. Each of the marriages began as a love affair, the first two based largely on sexual attraction, according to Lucretia: "I married the first two times for sex" (59), she says openly and without denying the power of the physical bond in a romantic affair. In the case of her most recent husband, Jason, however, their love endured even "after the early raptures of mutual discovery" wore off (61). Then Jason died of cancer after much suffering, but Lucretia remembers romantically and nostalgically "their trips. Lovely Italian wine and, at times, good sex" (61). In the present, Burt McElroy is pursuing her, though she is infatuated not with Burt but with an old acquaintance, Simon Coyne, now a Berkeley professor. There is about him "some hint of all the men she had ever loved" (72). When finally she convinces him to join her at her home for dinner, she exerts so much energy preparing food and drink for a romantic evening that when the time arrives she has to ask him if they can eat early because she is "sort of tired." Further putting a damper on the romantic mood, Simon admits that he also finds that he often becomes tired, and Lucretia decides at that moment that she will never think about falling in love again. In the story's final sentence the narrator reminds the reader, however, that this is impossible for Lucretia because of the persistence of the romantic impulse in her and those like her: "but of course she did [fall in love again]" (72).

"Great Sex," "The Haunted Beach," and "The Islands" also contain female main characters who, like Lucretia, remain open to romantic relationships after earlier ones have ended. In "Great Sex" Alison Green remains open to an emotional (and physical) attachment after the man she loves and is about to marry is killed by a hit-and-run driver. She falls in love, "all inner wisdom notwithstanding" (38), with Jack, a married man who lives in a distant city and has children. She becomes pregnant; has the child, Jennifer, rather than an abortion as Jack wishes her to do; and raises Jennifer as a single parent, refusing to cash occasional checks that Jack sends to help. After five years, while Jennifer is out of town visiting her grandmother, Alison encounters Jack in a restaurant with his wife, who is visiting San Francisco with him. He later calls Alison and comes alone to her house for a friendly visit, and she allows herself to be open again to him emotionally and sexually: after she cries as he is about to leave, "they begin to kiss, and minutes later they have moved to Alison's bedroom, where, on her bed, once more, they have great—the greatest sex" (45). Adams leaves the reader to decide whether her openness—some would perhaps say her romantic readiness in the face of yet another inevitable disappointment—is in her best interest in the long term.

In "The Haunted Beach" it is necessary for Penelope to revisit a West Mexican resort hotel in order to become free of her idealization of Charles, her former lover of five years—and of the illusion that San Bartolomeo was paradise. Before Penelope broke up with Charles, they had visited the island every year, and now that they are no longer together she has idealized it. In the present she brings her new lover, Ben, to San Bartolomeo, hoping to experience the magic she has known there in the past—and perhaps to experience new magic with Ben. But when they arrive, nothing seems the same to Penelope about her enchanted island, nor does it seem likely that she and Ben will be a good match for each other. Everything about the hotel she once stayed in with Charles and about the nearby town seems shabbier; the beach itself has lost its charm. After she returns to San Francisco, Penelope reports to her closest friend that "the trip made me feel a lot better. . . . About everything. More free" (35). The reason for her freedom was that ". . . I hardly thought about Charles. He wasn't there" (34). And she adds, "Actually I didn't think much about Ben either" (35). She has left behind that haunted beach, and this is a source of hope for Penelope in that she is now free to live in the present and look ahead "with a laugh" to the future (35). As it turned out, while she and Ben were there, her willingness to try again with him did not lead to a romantic bond, partly because Ben did not care much for San Bartolomeo, preferring to think of Hawaii, where he and his now-dead wife used to have good times together. Penelope is now apparently open to a new romantic relationship since she is finally detached from memories of Charles and also of Ben. The haunted beach remains where it was in San Bartolomeo as the story title suggests, but perhaps the point is that the beach no longer haunts Penelope.

"The Islands" also contains a main female character who, like Penelope, is attempting to try love again three years after the death of her husband, Andrew, whom she "really liked" and was "crazy about" (105) and about whose death she "was more grievous . . . than [she] can (or will) say" (109). Andrew and the narrator had shared a love both of Rome and of their cat, Pink, who in the present has just died. The narrator has cut short the grieving process over

Pink and taken a trip to Hawaii with her new lover, Slater, with whom she is attempting a relationship in spite of the fact that she was "not at all drawn to him" (106). The narrator knows that Andrew would not have liked Slater, and another thing that works against him in her eyes is that he is a developer and now on the verge of "developing" parts of "the islands," a fact that would have horrified the narrator's former friend, Zoe Pinkerton (now dead), a rich, alcoholic Texan from whom she and Andrew adopted Pink.

Zoe had an idealized love of Hawaii, which she referred to as "the islands" and to which she said she would move "if those grubby developers have kept their hands off of anything there" (113). Slater, of course, is one of those "grubby developers," and he proves himself not to be a cat lover, as he demonstrates when he and the narrator encounter several cats while in Hawaii. Back in San Francisco after having been deprived of a proper grieving process over Pink's death, the narrator begins to wonder why she went out with Slater, just as Slater, as the narrator imagines it, has begun to "wonder what we were doing together in the first place" (122). He heads back to Hawaii "to finish the ruination of all that was left of Zoe's islands" (122), and the narrator is left with "time alone . . . [to] think about Pink" (122), an ending that foregrounds the role animals can and do play in the emotional lives of animal lovers, who deal often with feelings about their love lives through projections onto pets. Adams explores this process in detail in two other stories in the first part of the volume: "Raccoons" and "A Very Nice Dog."

In "His Women" Adams treats the subject of being open to love after an unhappy romantic experience from an omniscient point of view with a focus on the central male character's perspective, rendering the story similar in one respect to "The Last Lovely City." The narrative focus in "His Women" is on Carter, a twice-rejected man in Chapel Hill. His first wife, Isabel, left him after having had affairs with various boyfriends in town, and then his second wife, Meredith, married him in the wake of Isabel's abandonment. But Meredith then falls in love with a fellow musician and leaves Carter for him. At this point, one might assume that Adams is developing Carter as a sympathetic character—one like all of those other rejected and/or abandoned lovers in the other stories in this part of the collection. In fact, Carter is not one of Adams's romantic heroes because he allows himself to become a victim. He refuses to dream or to imagine what he might do to empower himself. Instead, he drifts into another relationship with an independent artist (herself potentially an Alice Adams heroine) largely because she asserts herself. All the while Carter places himself at the mercy of the whims of the stock market and of his former wife Meredith, to whom he ultimately decides to return at her request because they are bound together by their shared mortgage on a house in which they had lived in together until she began an affair with her cellist boyfriend. Without a direct statement of disapproval, Adams creates in Carter the exemplary unsympathetic antihero—a person who refuses to dream, hope, or imagine a life beyond rejection. Unlike Zamora, one of numerous other heroic characters in the first part of *The Last Lovely City,* Chase is unwilling to take the initiative to raise a hand in shaping his own destiny.

"The Visit," which immediately precedes the title story in *The Last Lovely City,* is a bridge story between this volume and Adams's four earlier story collections. Although the unnamed town to which Grace Lafferty—a former Broadway actress and film star who is now mainly a television bit-part personality—returns is in the hill country of Georgia, the story is clearly patterned on the Hilton stories, one or more of which appears in every story collection published before *The Last Lovely City.* As is true of many of the Hilton stories in which the main female character typically grows up in the town, leaves it, and revisits it with complicated and mixed feelings later in life, Grace returns to her small Georgia hometown with a mixture of anticipation and anxiety. She has seldom returned since she became a celebrity; on one hand, she remembers it "as being the most beautiful [place] that she remembered . . .[a]nywhere" (82), but, on the other, she has unhappy memories of her "turbulent girlhood there, before she got so beautiful (dyed her hair blond) and famous" (82). "The Visit," therefore, is related to the Hilton stories through their shared concern with nostalgia and the various ways individuals use it.

The story is related to others in *The Last Lovely City* in that it deals with idealization, though it is idealization of a different sort from that in most of the other stories in the collection. In "The Visit" there are no characters suffering from recent losses of love and from feelings of abandonment, but the reader senses that Grace, Miles Henry (Grace's lifelong friend and for this occasion the manager of Grace's visit), and Jonathan Harding (Grace's lawyer and apparently a current and slightly younger suitor) are on the verge of having their ideals put to a test. There is a sense also that the town has idealized Grace—the local "girl" who has become famous: "almost everyone [in town] was somewhat excited, interested in [Grace's] visit" (82). Much of Grace's uneasiness and anxiety over her return, though expressed only indirectly in her careful attention to her makeup and appearance, comes from her realization (and fear) that, as a movie star past her prime, she will not fulfill the townspeople's expectations—that she will not live up to the ideal image that she suspects they have of her.

The high dramatic moment of the story comes when Grace, Miles, and Jonathan join the snobbish and catty ninety-two-year-old Miss Dabney for tea in her home. Miss Dabney tells a story in which Grace as a very young child sneaked under the table at her parents' dinner party and bit her mother on the ankle. According to Miss Dabney it was this act that has made the town proudest of Grace, since no one in town much cared for her mother, though all the women had crushes on her father. Miss Dabney seems surprised when Grace doesn't remember this biting episode, but in recounting it for Grace she manages both to downplay the town's pride in Grace's accomplishments as an actress and also to bring back memories that are painful to Grace. After pausing for a moment and not contradicting Miss Dabney, as would befit a talented actress who is also a Southern gentlewoman schooled not to contradict her elders, Grace, finally "abandoning all rules," responds to Miss Dabney's surprise that no one had recalled for her the story Miss Dabney has just narrated: "I guess up to now no one ever told me so as not to make me feel small and bad. I guess they knew I'd have to get very old and really mean before I'd think that was funny" (87). Through all of this, Jonathan, who is old enough that he has retired as a lawyer, begins to realize that "Grace is really too old for him but [her] fame he has enjoyed, up to a point" (87). In the story's last line, Miles, on the other hand, thinks, "Ah, that's my girl!"

The characters in "The Visit" are at different places in their lives. The reader does not know Miss Dabney's entire story, but on the basis of the description of her (covered with jewels with her head held erect by a heavy pearl choker) and her house (stuffed with silver frames, photographs, loveseats, and glassed-in bookcases, priceless objects everywhere), it appears that she has acquired and idealized material things, and they have brought only unhappiness. Jonathan clearly has idealized Grace's fame rather than Grace herself, and, though not much younger than Grace, he focuses on her advanced age, even as he apparently denies the inevitability of his own aging. Miles has idealized Grace for reasons hidden from people in the town and from the reader, but they seem anchored in an image of her from the past when she was a free-spirited "girl." This image has been reaffirmed by her response to Miss Dabney. Grace herself seems perhaps to be at a turning point in her life, and the question remains as to whether the nostalgic visit will aid her in confronting her idealized self-image. Having relied on her own success as an actress, she will soon, as the reader sees from the trajectory of her career, have to come to terms with its fragility, given her age and the nature of her profession. Her beautifully calculated, defiant response to Miss Dabney leaves the reader to question whether she has the capacity to become less the rebellious "girl" that Miles sees her as and more the liberated, independent, and individuated woman that Adams's heroines are at their best.

The four stories that constitute the relatively short Part Two of *The Last Lovely City* share characters whose lives are intertwined in such a way that, taken together, they form a novella of sorts that contains an episodic rendering of one of Adams's most complex and modern love stories. Viewed as a linear narrative, the story unfolds in this way: Julian Brownfield is a successful San Francisco psychiatrist married for more than two decades to Karen, a beautiful concert pianist (Wellesley and Julliard schooled) who is also an alcoholic. Karen continues to have affairs with other men throughout their marriage, is frequently clinically depressed, and often cancels concerts on a moment's notice, usually as a result of her having gone on a drinking binge. As a psychiatrist, Julian accepts the reality not only that he is drawn to Karen's extraordinary beauty but also that he is emotionally bound to her as an enabler of her alcoholism: he often reflects on her physical beauty, and he cannot resist coming to her aid when she is in another city on a concert tour and depressed or in morning-after despair over having canceled a concert after a night or day of drinking. He also always takes her back into his arms after she has strayed from him. Julian's real love, however, as it develops through the series of stories, is his former medical school friend, now a fellow psychiatrist and colleague in San Francisco, Lila Lewishohn, divorced early in the narrative by Garrett, who has abandoned her for his young pregnant girlfriend, Phyllis. Over the course of the four stories, there are, both for Julian and for Lila, painful separations from each other (even after both are divorced, technically free from their marriages), and there are periodic returns by Karen, for whom Julian continues to regard himself as caretaker. In the end—chronologically five years from the time of Julian's divorce from Karen—the reader does not learn how their stories will end and instead only grasps the fact that Julian and Lila's love is a constant, as Julian and Karen's seemingly permanent codependency is a reality.

As is true of so many of Adams's stories, a summary recounting of the narrative does a disservice to their accomplishment. This is especially true in the case of the four-story novella that concludes *The Last Lovely City,* the complexity of which lies, among other places, in Adams's cinematic rendering of each part of the narrative and in her artful use of the omniscient point of view, whose focus shifts seamlessly among the characters. In "The Drinking Club," the first story of the series, Karen's pattern of going off on an alcoholic binge that results in a last-minute concert cancellation is vividly rendered in prose that captures her disorientation: "Harsh, powerful sunlight strikes the far edge of the giant pink bed on which Karen Brownfield, a pianist, now lies alone, Karen on a concert tour. It must be midmorning, or nearly. On the other hand, perhaps early afternoon . . . . wherever she is now and whatever time it is, what day, she is not in Paris. Karen is sure of that much" (127). When she telephones Julian to tell him of the cancellation, his response, in part, is to feel guilt over not having gone with her to Atlanta—a fact that the reader learns when there is a narrative shift to San Francisco, to the bed where Julian and Lila have spent the night and where Julian takes the call from Karen in which she tells him of her cancellation.

In the second story, "Patients," the focus shifts to Lila and to her patience with Garrett's new wife, Phyllis, who has made an appointment with Lila under an assumed name so that she can learn more about her. Lila's patience is further highlighted during a visit from Garrett, ostensibly to discuss ways of helping Phyllis deal with her life with him. On this occasion he absurdly says to Lila, in the way of a serious proposal, "what I'd like would be to take you to bed. Right now" (152). Then, in a cinematic shift, Adams takes the reader into the hotel room in Maine where Julian and Karen are together during a time after the Atlanta "drinking club" episode and on a trip intended to help her with her alcoholism. Predictably, Karen slips off to Boston while Julian goes out for a swim, during which he worries that Karen might commit suicide. He returns with his dilemma, as he always does, to Lila in San Francisco, where he and Lila discuss Karen clinically. As always, Lila patiently listens even as she imagines various scenarios related to her future with Julian. She clearly loves him, but she also realizes that from the standpoint of their emotional health both of them must retain their individuality—must resist becoming codependent on each other.

In "The Wrong Mexico," which follows "Patients," Julian is in Mexico with Helen, an attractive blond he has met at his tennis club. He has imagined, during a temporary break in his relationship with Lila, that he might be "in love" with Helen, who is divorced from her alcoholic husband, has four children, and thinks she has finally met in Julian a man who finally might listen to her and be caring. For his part, Julian has quickly realized that he is not in love with Helen. He has in fact come to Mexico in search figuratively of Lila, who had vacationed alone there each winter during her marriage and during the time she and Julian were lovers. He sees now that he has "come to the wrong place with the wrong woman" (162). After Helen gracefully volunteers to leave and take a side trip to Oaxaca, Julian, in a deep depression, explores the surrounding area and finds the now-abandoned hotel where Lila had stayed and that she had described vividly to him. Contacting her by telephone to tell her of his discovery, he comes to see through her the value of his staying on in Mexico and treating his depression by walking, swimming, and reflecting on his situation as a psychiatrist determined to cure himself without giving in to his dependence on Lila.

In the final story of the series, "Earthquake Damage," it is Lila's turn to feel depressed and alone without Julian. She has been at a psychiatric conference on the contemporary state of being single, and, when the plane she is taking for her return to San Francisco experiences severe turbulence after takeoff, she sends up a prayer for help addressed to the following "odd bunch: to God, in whom she does not believe; to Freud, about whom she has serious doubts; to her old shrink, who is dead; and to her mother, also dead, whom she mostly did not like—and to her former (she supposes it is now former) lover, Julian Brownfield, also a shrink" (179). As it turns out, the plane has to return to Toronto after news comes that an earthquake has struck San Francisco. This makes it impossible for her to return until the airport there has been reopened.

The plane returns to Toronto, and passengers are housed at the Hilton as they await word that the San Francisco airport has reopened. Lila experiences near panic as she wonders about Julian's safety. As Lila waits in despair, Adams shifts the scene to San Francisco and to Julian's house in Mill Valley, where he is enduring Karen's rage at not being able to fly immediately out of San Francisco because of the earthquake. Five years after her divorce from Julian, she has returned, and Julian has taken her in once more. Now, though, she is packed and ready to leave yet again, though not before another vodka and orange juice binge in honor of the earthquake. Back in Toronto, with news that her plane will leave soon for San Francisco, Lila reaches Julian on the telephone, and he informs her that Karen will be leaving immediately. In the final scene of the story Lila is on the plane ready for takeoff, delayed only briefly by a dog on the runway, a detail that Lila immediately determines that she will share with Julian when she is back in San Francisco. It appears that Lila's prayer to that "odd bunch" has been answered, at least in part. Instead of feeling the despair at her sense of isolation that she had experienced during the turbulence after the initial takeoff, she now is hopeful: she imagines that she will share the story of the runway dog with Julian, indicating that she anticipates a reunion. An important detail that helps contextualize the publication of the last four stories is that they actually preceded the publication of the others in *The Last Lovely City:* the first story in the group, "The Drinking Club," published in the *New Yorker* in 1987, is the earliest of the stories in the collection, and "Earthquake Damage," the last of the four, appeared in the *New Yorker* in 1990, the year before the magazine published "The Last Lovely City." As noted earlier, the last years of the 1980s (and the decade in general) were years of discouragement for Adams. The 1990s offered new hope, and this hope is reflected in the renewed faith in romantic idealism evident in "Earthquake Damage" and even more obviously in "The Last Lovely City." This hope remains alive and well in *A Southern Exposure* (1995) and in the posthumous *After the War* (2000), the novel that Adams was completing at the time of her death.

CHAPTER 8

Posthumous

After the War

In 1995 Adams had published *A Southern Exposure* and in 1997 *Medicine Men,* both drawing on details from her own experiences—the former from her personal knowledge of the South and the latter from her recent illness and her observations about the medical establishment as well as the culture of San Francisco. After the publication of *Medicine Men,* she began making entries in an "After the War" notebook, indicating that by this time she was thinking seriously about the novel that would become a sequel to *A Southern Exposure,* which is set—as *After the War* (2000) is set—in the fictional town of Pinehill, near Hilton (based on Chapel Hill). In April 1998, on the occasion of the North Carolina Literary Festival, she made what would be her final trip to Chapel Hill, spending two nights there with her longtime friend Max Steele and then moving to the Carolina Inn, which she calls by name in *After the War.* Adams died on May 27, 1999, slightly more than a year after her last Chapel Hill trip. Following the posthumous publication of *After the War,* in 2000, Sybil Steinberg made this observation in a *Publisher's Weekly* review: "Reading this posthumous novel is a bittersweet experience. On the one hand, it's wonderful to be back in the Southern town of Pinehill, and to enjoy Adams's inimitable prose and her calm intimacy with the characters introduced in *A Southern Exposure.* On the other, it's a pity to realize that we'll never know what future lives Adams had planned for these vibrant individuals."[1]

All readers who care for Adams's work likely share the sentiment about the bittersweet experience of reading *After the War* while knowing it is Adams's last work. Steinberg's words would likely have brought an ironic gleam to Adams's eyes. They suggest that she had planned future lives for these characters. This would suggest that she had "plotted out" a novel or stories to follow *After the War,* but, as Adams made clear to Jack Leggett slightly more than a month before her death, "I don't care for plot at all."[2] This leads to one of the important points to carry away from *After the War* as it is read in association with *A Southern Exposure:* it is the way the characters respond to the events that take place over the course of the two novels—and the way Adams observes their responses, her "calm intimacy with the characters"—rather than the events themselves, that are of primary significance in both novels. In *A Southern Exposure* Adams's central concern is with characterization, with the process by which three main sets of characters—the Baird family, the Byrd family, and the Pinehill townspeople around them—develop, given the circumstances of their lives over the course of a five-year period 1939–1944, a period marked at the beginning by the lull before the United States entered World War II and at the end by the summer of the year before the bombing of Hiroshima and Nagasaki, which led to the Japanese surrender in 1945.

Adams builds *After the War* on the foundation she established in *A Southern Exposure,* particularly regarding a generally progressive shift in the attitudes of Pinehill residents regarding gender and racial equality, a shift evident especially in those strands of the narrative involving Cynthia, Abby, and some of their formerly sexist and racist friends. It becomes clear almost from the beginning of *After the War* that Adams had ambitious plans for extending her observations about social injustice in America outward beyond Pinehill, largely through Cynthia and Abby, and for constructing the novel around three major subjects that were important to Adams not only in *A Southern Exposure* but also in virtually all of her novels from the beginning of her career. The subjects are gender, racial, and ethnic inequality, all three of which are addressed in *After the War* on both regional and national levels. Adams also, through her resonant title and mainly at the level of subtext, extends these subjects back across three of America's major wars—the Civil War, World War I, and World War II—all of which have been directly or indirectly involved to some degree in the struggle for civil rights, whether gender, racial, or ethnic equality; when the ubiquitous phrase "after the war" is uttered in the novel, as it is throughout, one could legitimately inquire as to which war is being referred to—and also raise questions about the degree of social change that came about after each war.

Adams first orients readers of *After the War* through a party at the Bairds' pool, a gathering reminiscent of the one in the closing scene of *A Southern Exposure.* Harry, because he is in London in the midst of the fighting, is absent from this second party, as is one of the local men who has died during the period of more than a year that separates the two parties, this one in *After the War* intended to celebrate the departure of Abby for Swarthmore and

Melanctha, daughter of Russ and Sally Jane, for Radcliffe. The children are growing up and moving away from Pinehill and out into the world. Cynthia "during the war" is described as "an actively unfaithful Navy wife" (3). She is presently exercising her temporary freedom from marriage by having a secret affair with a famous war correspondent, Derek, and she hopes he will call while the party is in progress. The guests, most of whom were pictured to be in good form at the earlier pool party in *A Southern Exposure,* have changed, if only slightly, to the observant eye, since that time. Cynthia, for one, is glad none of the adults, particularly the women, have worn their bathing suits, as they did for the last gathering: "They're mostly too old and too fat, a lot of them. Dolly Bigelow is very plump, and her husband, Willard, too; Deirdre Byrd is truly fat (could she possibly be pregnant again?)" (7). The men look somewhat better to Cynthia, though she imagines how much better Harry would look than any of them in his "Navy things," as would Derek in his war-correspondent "belted trench coat, with his pipe" (7). As was true at the earlier party, most of those in attendance at the present one seem nearly oblivious to the fact that the deadliest war in history is in progress in Europe. Cynthia, for example, thinks of Harry's being overseas and of the war in much the way everyone in Pinehill does: "Harry and wartime London, as well as the war itself, were vague to Cynthia, as they were to most of the rest of that town" (3).

With this party Cynthia, absent and in Georgetown much of the a time since the last party, reestablishes herself for the reader and the guests as a member in good standing of the social world of Pinehill and as a champion of women's rights, not only because she has publically proven herself acceptable to a prestigious, presumably gender-blind law school but also because she has chosen privately to have a love affair with Derek while her husband is out of the country in London, exercising (she assumes) his right, as well, to have a relationship outside their marriage. Earlier she had carried on a long-dreamed-of affair with her romantic hero, Russell Byrd, while Harry was away in Washington; in the end, she chose to turn down his proposal of marriage on the valid assumption that neither of them wanted to be married to the other, though each loved the other.

Her relationship with Derek allows the reader to understand Cynthia's character, particularly the way in which she has evolved (and is evolving) into the Alice Adams woman, familiar to readers of Adams's work from *Careless Love* forward: she is a strong, intelligent, attractive, independent woman, but she is also, and as importantly, a romantic idealist—a person who believes that there is such a thing as love and that it is to be honored in most cases over pragmatic considerations, including one's marriage. And it is worth the risk of pain. Cynthia's romanticism comes into high relief in her relationship with Derek when he tells her, "I never fall in love. I'm not a romantic like you, I try hard for realism" (32). As she tries to protest what she knows to be true, he goes on to say, "you're so romantic about—everything" (33). He is right, of course, and though she likes to see herself strictly as "the modern, sophisticated woman" (34), she remains the romantic idealist who is also a "modern, sophisticated woman," a combination of qualities evident in the most admirable of Adams's female characters. They are strong, and yet they are not immune to feelings of extraordinary passion or deep pain when love affairs do not work out. Cynthia is such a woman and has been at least from the time she persuaded Harry to move to Pinehill so that she could be near Russ Byrd, though she does not tell Harry the reason. She remains a romantic until the end of the novel, at which time she still aches from the lost love she felt for Russ and then Derek, both of whose romantic relationships with Deirdre brought her deep pain.

By the end of the novel she has been accepted (again) into Georgetown's law school and plans to return to the area to live with Harry, though the reader is led at the end to believe she is not closing off the possibility that a new love could come into her life. Her willingness to remain vulnerable to the pain that often accompanies love seems not to keep her from requiring equality in her relationships with men and from standing up to the patriarchal establishment, challenging gender discrimination whenever she encounters it. Worth noting is that Cynthia, born in 1907 and thus almost a teenager when the armistice that ended World War I was signed, is acting in the spirit of the progressive women of her generation. In the wake of that war, when Cynthia was thirteen, Congress ratified the Nineteenth Amendment, giving women the right to vote. The ratification was thought by many to have been a result of the extraordinary efforts by women during the war; thus "after the war" the position of women was better than before the war. The Equal Rights Amendment was first introduced, though never ratified, in Congress in 1923, during Cynthia's sixteenth year. When she protested her rejection by the Hilton law school, a result, they tell her, of her being a woman and also too old to study law, the patriarchs responsible should not have been surprised by her response. Her protest was in keeping with the feminist spirit of her times: "those dumb jerks at Hilton. . . . Just wait till I get my degree at Georgetown or even Harvard! I think they let in 'ladies' at Harvard, Yale too" (282). Neither Hilton nor Pinehill was there yet.

Abby, for her part, becomes the champion of civil rights for African Americans from the moment the Bairds move to Pinehill at the beginning of *A Southern Exposure* through the end of *After the War*. She has brought with her from Connecticut her memories of a close friendship with her African American classmate Ben Davis from her early school years, and as a teenager she had written a research paper on integration, detailed in *A Southern Exposure*, that indirectly challenged the Jim Crow mentality of Pinehill residents and marked her as an extremist at an early age. Now, in *After the War,* as a student at Swarthmore, she maintains her friendship with Ben and introduces him to the family of Joseph Marcus, her Jewish boyfriend from New York. Joseph's mother and father are members of the Communist Party, and when Abby introduces them to Ben they immediately attempt to recruit him into the Party since he is an intelligent, handsome African American, also an excellent student and a football player at Harvard. He would add prestige and diversity to the Party—not to mention glory to the name of Joseph's father. In one of Ben's conversations with Abby after he has met the Marcus family and gained insight into their personalities, he tells Abby what to him was an "interesting, and sort of ironic" (46) story that has bearing on his present status as a Harvard student and prospective recruit for virtually any organization in America, including the Communist Party. His grandfather, a slave in the Deep South before the Civil War, had escaped to the North through the Underground Railroad and had been one of the first African Americans to own land in Connecticut. He had left the acre he bought to Ben's father, and after the Depression the government needed to build a Navy base on land that included Davis's acre. In extended negotiations with what the government, which likely assumed it was dealing with "a sentimental, stubborn old colored man" (46), Ben's father agreed to part with his acre for a sizable amount of money that included enough for a new cottage elsewhere and a lifetime pension for Ben's mother. After two wars—the Civil War and World War I—and with a third about to begin—World War II—the land of a former slave had, in part, made it possible for Ben to become a Connecticut Yankee at Harvard. The Marcus family, of course, had no reason to know any of this, and it becomes, in Ben's words, "interesting, and somewhat ironic" to consider the implications of his story: Joseph, a Jewish man from New York who doesn't subscribe to his parents' Communist ideology, and Ben's friend Abby, a displaced Connecticut Yankee turned Southerner, become the instruments of exposure—at least to the reader—of the racism implicit in Ben's treatment at the hand of Joseph's ostensibly "anti-racist" parents. And, in another ironic twist, the reverse-racist attitudes of the Marcus family become more evident when, again through Abby and her Swarthmore classmate Susan Marcus, Joseph's sister, the Marcus family plays a role in rescuing the African American Ed Faulkner from a possible lynching after he has been accused of complicity in the death of Russ Byrd when both are on a train headed East from California. Russ dies of a heart attack in the presence of Ed, and since the train is in a racist area in Texas when Russ dies, Ed, because he is African American, is jailed and wrongly accused of killing Russ. Through their Party connections, the Marcus family is able to bring him back East, and eventually they take him in as a family member, all the while having little conscious understanding of the complex dynamics of their reverse racism, which is at once well meaning and also condescending.

Through Abby, then, the multiracial, multiethnic world of the northeastern United States comes to intersect with that of the mid-South. As Abby's friendship with Benny continues and her relationship with Joseph progresses toward engagement and marriage, Abby introduces the African American Benny and the Jewish Joseph into the provincial society of Pinehill. One obvious consequence of Abby's belief in racial equality becomes evident in her introduction of her friend Melanctha to Ben, with whom Melanctha openly forms a close emotional bond, one that seems likely to people in town (and to the reader) to be leading toward a romantic relationship. Also, in matters of religion and ethnicity Abby has been steadfast in her acceptance of those whose ethnicities or religious beliefs are different from hers: her relationship with a Jewish man, for example, presents a challenge to Pinehill residents, whose anti-Semitic sentiments before the war have seemed to lie barely beneath the surface of their Southern, mostly white Anglo-Saxon Protestant personas. The war, after all, has been fought against Nazi Germany and was, at least in part, an effort on the part of the United States to eliminate discrimination against the Jewish people. With the war won by the time of Abby and Joseph's wedding, a large step has been taken nationally in the direction of combating anti-Semitism, and the presence of a diverse crowd for the wedding celebration seems an optimistic sign.

At the gathering for the wedding and the festivities around it, there is interaction among individuals who would likely not have been together as comfortably at a social function before the war. A local Presbyterian minister, a "liberal radical," conducts the ceremony with a rabbi from Hilton in attendance. Also, Graham, the gay son of Russ and Deirdre, has come down from Harvard with his partner, Paxton Sedgwick. Joseph's mother, Sylvia, has come in from New York. Others attending the celebration include various members of the Pinehill community, most representative among them Cynthia's friend Dolly Bigelow, who arranged the pre-wedding party. In such a diverse group there are inevitably differences based on long-standing prejudices related to race, ethnicity, gender, and religious beliefs, and predictably there is evidence that these differences, existing from long "before the war," have not entirely vanished: the Episcopal minister, for example, had refused to conduct the ceremony because Joseph had not been "christened" (295). Also, there is typical Pinehill small-town gossip: "And how about that Melanctha? You imagine that little old girl off in Montana or Texas either with a bunch of dogs? . . . And maybe a colored boyfriend" (293).

In spite of these differences, the atmosphere, largely thanks to the mediating force of Abby in particular, is cordial—even warmly celebratory. At least during the celebration of this union of a Jewish, Northern man and an almost local, progressive Pinehill young woman, the town seems after the war to be a more tolerant and accepting place than it was before. At the novel's end, Dolly Bigelow provides a gentle reminder that there is progress yet to be made. In her patronizing, all-knowing conversation with Odessa, Cynthia and Harry's housekeeper and formerly Dolly's "colored help," she knowingly informs Odessa that, on the basis of her observations of Cynthia and Harry's warm interactions, she has determined that they will be renewing their vows today. Odessa's reply reflects her wisdom, her restraint, and her knowledge of Cynthia. It also leaves open-ended for the reader the future of Cynthia's romantic idealism as Odessa closes *After the War* with a question whose answer will never be known for certain: "You reckon?" (305).

It is fitting that Adams ended her last novel on a note of hope, which has from the beginning of her professional career been a trademark of her work and of her life. Cynthia, who is of Adams's mother's generation, has struggled through the years of *A Southern Exposure* and *After the War* to find her identity in the social sphere free from constructions of gender that have been determined by the patriarchy, and in this she has largely been successful. She has gained the freedom to choose whether to have a relationship with Harry, whether or not they are bound together in marriage by a legal document. With her acceptance into law school there is reasonable hope that she will take the next step and gain independence in the economic sphere as well—a step that would free her from any financial dependence on Harry or on any other man. And there is even greater hope for Abby, who at a relatively early age has found in Joseph a man who is committed to a relationship in which both partners are equal. She is preparing for a career in medicine, which will bring her independence in the economic as well the domestic sphere. In a broader sense it is perhaps of even greater importance that Cynthia and Abby, who is of Adams's own generation, have both achieved their independence in a world that is, if gradually, becoming a world that is beginning to understand the importance of equality for all. When Adams died peacefully in the spring of 1999, she left her hopes for the next millennium to a new generation.

NOTES

Chapter 1: Understanding Alice Adams

1. This manuscript is archived in the Alice Adams Papers in the Harry Ransom Center, University of Texas at Austin. The notation "collected papers" will indicate future references to items in this collection.

2. Kay Bonetti, "Interview with Alice Adams," 1987, audio recording, American Audio Prose Library, Columbia, Mo.

3. Michael Silverblatt, "Bookworm," 1989, KCRW (Los Angeles), audio recording in collected papers.

4. Alice Adams, "At First Sight: Love and Liking, a Memoir," *Southern Review* 35, no. 3 (Summer 1999): 567.

5. Ibid., 574.

6. Alice Adams, "Summer, Clothes & Love," *San Francisco Examiner,* June 10, 1990, 30.}

7. Adams's fictional account of the love affair of this summer appeared as "Learning to Be Happy," *Redbook* 147, no. 1 (September 1976): 100, 141, 143, 145, 148–49, and was collected as "Home Is Where" in *Beautiful Girl,* 153–70. Steele's version of the relationship appeared as "About Love and Grasshoppers" in *Redbook* 149, no. 1 (May 1977): 126–27. 206–12, and was collected as "Another Love Story" in *The Hat of My Mother,*" 69–90.

8. Don Swaim, "Interview," September 17, 1984, audio recording available through Archives and Special Collections, Ohio University, Donald L. Swaim Collection.

9. Alice Adams, *Beautiful Girl* (New York: Knopf, 1979), 154.

10. Grover Sales, "A Boswell of Our Neurotic Intelligentsia," *Los Angeles Times,* January 29, 1978, 1m.

11. Bonetti, "Interview."

12. Ibid.

13. "Memorial Service," June 27, 1999, audio recording in collected papers.

14. Ibid.

15. Annie Gottlieb, "They Stumbled Blindly into Marriage: *Families and Survivors,*" *New York Times,* March 16, 1975, sec. 7, 29.

16. Adams, July 11, 1973, in Alfred A. Knopf, Inc., Records, located in the Harry Ransom Center, University of Texas at Austin. The notation "Knopf Records" will indicate future reference to these records.

17. Gottlieb, "They Stumbled Blindly into Marriage: *Families and Survivors,*" 28.

Chapter 2: The Early Novels

1. F. Scott Fitzgerald, *This Side of Paradise,* ed. James L. W. West III (New York: Cambridge University Press, 1995), 219.

2. Beverly Lowry, "Women Who Know Better," *New York Times Book Review,* September 1, 1985, 5.

3. Mildred Hamilton, "It's a Very Good Year for Alice," *San Francisco Examiner,* January 31, 1975, 22.

4. Swaim, "Interview," September 17, 1984.

5. Victoria Wilson to Alice Adams, July 11, 1973, letter, Knopf Records.

6. Margaret Manning, "The Tragedy Is Muted," *Boston Globe,* January 20, 1975, 24.

7. Patricia Holt, "Alice Adams," *Publisher's Weekly* (January 16, 1978), 8.

8. Ibid.

9. Cara Chell, "Succeeding in Their Times: Alice Adams on Women and Work," *Soundings: An Interdisciplinary Journal* 68 (Spring 1985): 66.

Chapter 3: Early Stories

1. Neil Feineman, "An Interview with Alice Adams," *StoryQuarterly* no. 11 (1980): 35.

2. Grover Sales, "A Boswell of the Neurotic Intelligentsia," *Los Angeles Times,* January 29, 1978, M1.

3. Patricia Holt, "A Banquet of Riches—Mostly in the Moody City," *San Francisco Sunday Examiner & Chronicle,* February 4, 1979, 47.

4. Susan Wood, "Stories of Love and Loss," *Washington Post Magazine,* January 21, 1979, G3. Wood here is quoting Trilling.

5. Ibid.

6. Bonetti, "Interview."

7. Victoria Wilson to Alice Adams, letter, July 11, 1973, Knopf Records.

8. Lee Upton, "Changing the Past: Alice Adams' Revisionary Nostalgia," *Studies in Short Fiction* 26, no. 1 (Winter 1989): 34.

9. Beverly Lowry, "Women Who Know Better," *New York Times Book Review,* September 1, 1985, 5.

Chapter 4: 1980s Novels

1. Larry T. Blades, "Order and Chaos in Alice Adams' *Rich Rewards,*" *Critique: Studies in Contemporary Fiction* 27 (Summer 1986): 187.

2. Larry Rumley, "'Rich Rewards': Decorator's Loves Grow Complex," *Seattle Times,* November 23, 1980, F8.

3. Blades fully explores the idea of the triumph of "chaos" and decadence in the novel in "Order and Chaos in Alice Adams' *Rich Rewards,*" 187–95.

4. Roberta Smoodin, "Alice Adams' Breakthrough Novel," *Los Angeles Herald Examiner,* September 2, 1984, G5.

5. Ibid., G6.

6. Phil Thomas, "Writers Need Aid, Author Says," *Seattle Post-Intelligencer,* May 3, 1982, D6.

7. Alex Madrigal, "The Breaking of a Mold," *San Francisco Chronicle,* September 9, 1984, 11.

8. Terry Trucco, "The First 'Alice Adams Woman,'" *International Herald Tribune,* February 18, 1983, 7W.

9. Diana Ketcham, "Superior Women's Plight Is Novel's Theme," *Oakland Tribune,* September 12, 1984, E-1, E-3.

10. See "Superior Women, by Alice Adams," *Los Angeles Times,* September 30, 1984, WBK1.

11. Nancy Pate, "'Women' Authentic Slice of Life," *Wichita Eagle* (Kansas), September 23, 1984, 5F.

12. Nancy Connors, "Sexual Desires Still Simmering in Twilight Years," *Cleveland Plain Dealer,* April 17, 1988, 1-H, 8-H.

13. Tom Dowling, "'Chances' Is Poignant Portrayal of Aging," *San Francisco Examiner,* May 5, 1988, C1.

14. Ibid.

Chapter 5: 1980s Stories

1. Phil Thomas, "Writers Need Aid, Author Says," *Seattle Post-Intelligencer,* May 3, 1982, D6.

2. Judith McConnell Steele, "'New Yorker' Veteran Shares Writing Tips," *Idaho Statesman,* February 14, 1982, 5C.

3. Millicent Dillon, "Writer Alice Adams Cuts to the Core in Her Fiction and in Her Reading," *Campus Report,* June 9, 1982, 9.

4. Ibid.

5. Ibid.

6. Elizabeth Forsythe Hailey, "Alice Adams: Mixing Entertainment and Insights," *Dallas Morning News,* May 2, 1982, 4G.

7. Ibid.

8. Lee Upton, "Changing Past: Alice Adams' Revisionary Nostalgia," *Studies in Short Fiction* 26, no. 1 (Winter 1989): 34.

9. Victoria Middleton, Review of *To See You Again, Southern Humanities Review* (Summer 1983): 289.

10. Linda Pastan, Review of *To See You Again, American Book Review* (July 1983): 4.

11. Dillon, "Writer Alice Adams Cuts to the Core," 9.

12. Ibid.

13. Ibid.

14. Patricia Holt, "Adams' Return Trip," *San Francisco Chronicle,* October 29, 1995, 1, 11.

15. Susan Walker, "Adams Can't Avoid Battle of the Sexes," *Toronto Star,* October 16, 1989, C4.

16. Ibid.

17. Bruce Cook, "She Won't Give Short Shrift to Short Stories," *Daily News LA Life,* October 25, 1989, L10.

18. Ibid.

19. Ibid.

Chapter 6: 1990s Novels

1. Carol Fowler, "New Novel Attacks Values of 1980s," *West County Times* (Contra Costa, Calif.), May 7, 1991, 3C.

2. Gail Boyer, "A Lusty Family Saga of Self-Indulgence," *St. Louis Post-Dispatch,* April 7, 1991, 5D.

3. Nancy Pearl, "A Southern Exposure," *Booklist,* August 1995, 1907, Literature Resource Center, http://go.galegroup/com/ps/i.do? (accessed May 6, 2017).

4. Joan Smith, "Ask Alice," *San Francisco Examiner Magazine,* October 22, 1995, 13.

5. Alice Adams, "A Shadow on the Brain," *Allure,* September 1993, 209.

6. Deborah Mason, "Poking and Prodding," *New York Times,* April 13, 1997, http://www.nytimes.com/1997/04/13/books/poking-and-prodding.html (accessed May 5, 2017).

7. Elisabeth Sherwin, "Adams Gives a Reading, Encourages Others to Write," *Davis Virtual Market,* July 14, 1996, http://dcn.davis.ca.us/~gizmo/alice.html (accessed February 17, 2018).

8. Ibid.

Chapter 7: 1990s Stories

1. *The Great Gatsby,* ed. Matthew J. Bruccoli (New York: Cambridge University Press, 1991), 140.

2. Ibid.

Chapter 8: Posthumous

1. Sybil Steinberg, Review of *After the War, Publishers Weekly* (August 14, 2000), 329.

2. "Memorial Service," June 27, 1999, collected papers.

BIBLIOGRAPHY

Works by Alice Adams

BOOKS

Careless Love. New York: New American Library, 1966. Republished as *The Fall of Daisy Duke.* London: Constable, 1967.
Families and Survivors. New York: Knopf, 1974.
Listening to Billie. New York: Knopf, 1978.
Beautiful Girl. New York: Knopf, 1979.
Rich Rewards. New York: Knopf, 1980.
To See You Again. New York: Knopf, 1982.
Molly's Dog. Concord, N.H.: Ewert, 1983.
Superior Women. New York: Knopf, 1984.
Return Trips. New York: Knopf, 1985.
Second Chances. New York: Knopf, 1988.
After You've Gone. New York: Knopf, 1989.
Mexico: Some Travels and Some Travelers There. New York: Prentice Hall, 1990.
Caroline's Daughters. New York: Knopf, 1991.
Almost Perfect. New York: Knopf, 1993.
A Southern Exposure. New York: Knopf, 1995.
Medicine Men. New York: Knopf, 1997.
The Last Lovely City. New York: Knopf, 1999.
After the War. New York: Knopf, 2000.
The Stories of Alice Adams. New York. Knopf, 2002.

SELECTED ESSAYS

"At First Sight: Love and Liking, a Memoir." *Southern Review* (Summer 1999): 567–78.
"Madeline and Me." *Life* 13(July 1990), 103.
"A Shadow on the Brain." *Allure* (September 1993): 170–73, 209.
"Summer, Clothes & Love: A Memoir by Alice Adams." *Image* (June 10,1990): 25–26, 28–31.

INTERVIEWS

Bonetti, Kay. "Interview with Alice Adams." American Audio Prose Library, June 1987.
Feineman, Neil. "An Interview with Alice Adams." *StoryQuarterly* no. 11 (1980): 27–37.
Holt, Patricia. "PW Interviews: Alice Adams." *Publishers Weekly* 213 (January 16, 1978), 8–9.

Silverblatt, Michael. "Bookworm." KCRW (Los Angeles), October 16, 1989. Collected Alice Adams Papers, Harry Ransom Center at the University of Texas at Austin.

Swaim, Don. "Book Beat." Interviews with Alice Adams, September 17, 1984. Donald L. Swaim Collection, Ohio University Archives and Special Collections.

Thomas, Phil. "Writers Need Aid Author Says." *Seattle Post-Intelligencer,* May 3, 1982, D6.

COLLECTED PAPERS

Adams, Alice. The Harry Ransom Center. The University of Texas at Austin.

Works about Alice Adams

SELECTED WORKS

Barnes, Joanna. "The Loneliness of the Later Intimacies." Review of *Second Chances. Los Angeles Times,* May 8, 1988, 13.

Blades, Larry T. "Order and Chaos in Alice Adams' *Rich Rewards.*" *Critique: Studies in Modern Fiction* 27 (Summer 1986): 187–95.

Boston, Anne. A review of *Return Trips. Times Literary Supplement,* no. 4322, January 31, 1986, 112.

Boyer, Gail. "A Lusty Family Saga of Self-Indulgence." *St. Louis Post-Dispatch,* April 7, 1991, 5D.

Buchanan, William. A review of *To See You Again. Studies in Short Fiction* 20, nos. 2–3 (Spring–Summer 1983): 143.

Carlson, Ron. "Clobbering Her Ex." *New York Times Book Review,* October 8, 1989, 27.

Chell, Cara, "Succeeding in Their Times: Alice Adams on Women and Work." *Soundings: An International Journal* 68 (Spring 1985): 62–81.

Connors, Nancy. "Sexual Desires Still Simmering in Twilight Years." *Cleveland Plain Dealer,* April 17, 1988, 1-H, 8-H.

Cook, Bruce. "She Won't Give Short Shrift to Short Stories." *Daily News LA Life,* October 25, 1989, L9, L10.

DeMott, Benjamin. "Stories of Change." Review of *To See You Again. New York Times Book Review,* April 11, 1982, 7, 17.

Dillon, Millicent. "Writer Alice Adams Cuts to the Core in Her Fiction and in Her Reading." *Campus Report,* June 9, 1982. 9.

Dowling, Tom. "Breaking Stride in Homestretch of Life Is Hard to Do." *San Francisco Examiner,* May 5, 1988, C1.

Drewes, Caroline. "The Next Chapter." *San Francisco Examiner,* October 25, 1989, B1, B5.

Faber, Nancy. "Out of the Pages." *People* 9 (April 3, 1978), 48–9.

Ferguson, Christine. "Alice Adams." In *Dictionary of Literary Biography,* vol. 234: *American Short-Story Writers Since World War II, Third Series,* edited by Patrick Meanor, 3–15. Detroit: Gale, 2001.

Flower, Dean. "Picking Up the Pieces." *Hudson Review* 32, no. 2 (Summer 1979): 293–307.

Fowler, Carol. "New Novel Attacks Values of 1980s." *West County Times* (Contra Costa, Calif.), May 7, 1991, 3C.

Freleigh, Becky. "3 Women Turn Different Pages." *Cleveland Plain Dealer,* April 22, 1988. 14B.

Gottlieb, Annie. "They Stumbled Blindly into Marriage, Families and Survivors." Review of *Families and Survivors. New York Times,* March 16, 1975, 7, 28–9.

Hamilton, Mildred. "It's a Very Good Year for Alice." *San Francisco Examiner,* January 31, 1975, 22.

Harvey, John. "Love under the Knife." Review of *Medicine Men. Northern California's Complete Literary Guide Book Review,* April 6, 1997, 10.

Herman, Barbara A. "Alice Adams." In *Contemporary Fiction Writers of the South: A Bio-Bibliographical Sourcebook,* edited by Joseph M. Flora and Robert Bain, 11–21. Westport, Conn.: Greenwood Press, 1993.

Holt, Patricia. "A Banquet of Riches—Mostly in the Moody City." Review of *Beautiful Girl. San Francisco Sunday Chronicle,* February 4, 1979, 47.

———. "Adams' Return." *San Francisco Chronicle,* September 8, 1985, Sunday Review section, 1.

Johnson, Greg. "Some Recent Herstories." *Georgia Review* 44, nos. 1–2 (Spring–Summer 1990): 278–88.

Kakutani, Michiko. "Books of the Times." Review of *Return Trips. New York Times,* August 21, 1985, C17.

Ketcham, Diana. "Superior Women Is Novel's Theme," *Oakland Tribune,* September 12, 1984, E-1, E-3.

Kline, Betsy. "The Fine Line That Makes and Breaks Relationships." Review of *The Last Lovely City. Pittsburg Post-Gazette,* Washington (Pa.) edition, April 4, 1999, G8.

Lowry, Beverly. "Women Who Know Better." *New York Times Book Review,* September 1, 1985, 5.

Madrigal, Alix. "The Breaking of a Mold." *San Francisco Chronicle Review,* September 9, 1984, 11.

Manning, Margaret. "The Tragedy Is Muted." Review of *Families and Survivors. Boston Globe,* January 20, 1975, 24.

Mason, Deborah. "Poking and Prodding." *New York Times,* April 13, 1997. http://www.nytimes.com/1997/04/13/books/poking-and-prodding.html (accessed May 5, 2017).

Middleton, Victoria. Review of *To See You Again. Southern Humanities Review* (Summer 1983): 288–92.

Pastan, Linda. Review of *To See You Again. American Book Review,* July 1983, 4.

Pate, Nancy. "'Women' Authentic Slice of Life." *Wichita Eagle,* September 23, 1984, 5F.

Pearl, Nancy. "A Southern Exposure." *Booklist,* August 1995, 1907. Literature Resource Center, http://go.galegroup/com/ps/i.do? (accessed May 6, 2017).

Petroski, Catherine. "Tales of Broken Women: Deserted Women and Self-Absorbed Men Fill the Stories of Alice Adams." Review of *After You've Gone. Chicago Tribune,* September 3, 1989, 5.

Phelps, Teresa. "Alice Adams's Short Stories 'Make Sense.'" Review of *Return Trips. Chicago Tribune Book World,* September 1, 1985, 31.

Pollit, Katha. "Good Ole Boys and Wistful Hippies." Review of *Beautiful Girl. New York Times Book Review,* January 14, 1979, 14.

St. Andrews, B. A. Review of *A Southern Exposure. World Literature Today* 70, no. 3 (1996): 689.

See, Caroline. "Spoiled in Paradise." *Washington Post,* March 10, 1991, WBK1.

Sherwin, Elisabeth. "Adams Gives a Reading, Encourages Others to Write." *Davis Virtual Market,* July 14, 1996. http://dcn.davis.ca.us/~gizmo/alice.html (accessed February 17, 2018).

Showalter, Elaine. "Rethinking the Seventies: Women Writers and Violence." *Antioch Review* 39, no. 2 (Spring 1981): 156–70.

Smith, Joan. "Ask Alice." *San Francisco Examiner,* October 22, 1995, 12–15.

Smoodin, Roberta. "Rewards of Alice Adams." Review of *Rich Rewards. Los Angeles Herald Examiner,* September 28, 1980, F5.

Steele, Judith McConnell. "'New Yorker' Veteran Shares Writing Tips." *Idaho Statesman,* February 14, 1982, 5C.

Steele, Max. *The Hat of My Mother.* Chapel Hill: Algonquin Books, 1994.

Steinberg, Sybil. Review of *After the War. Publishers Weekly,* August 14, 2000, 329.

Trucco. Terry. "The First 'Alice Adams Woman,'" *International Herald Tribune,* February 18, 1983, Weekend Section, 7W.

Upton, Lee. "Changing Past: Alice Adams' Revisionary Nostalgia." *Studies in Short Fiction* 26, no. 1 (Winter 1989): 33–41.

Warga, Wayne. "A Sophisticated Author Gets By with Help from Her Friends." *Los Angeles Times Book Review,* November 16, 1980, 3.

Walker, Susan. "Adams Can't Avoid Battle of the Sexes." *Toronto Star,* October 16, 1989, C4.

Williamson, Barbara. "Aging without the Rage: Fiction of Old Friends Confronting Change." Review of *Second Chances. Washington Post,* May 6, 1988, B4.

Wilson, Victoria to Alice Adams, July 11, 1973. Alfred A. Knopf Records, Harry Ransom Center at The University of Texas at Austin.

Wood, Susan. "Stories of Love and Loss." Review of *Beautiful Girl. Washington Post Magazine,* January 21, 1979, G3.

INDEX